Price Per Barrel

Price Per Barrel

The Human Cost of Extraction

By Robin Lynn Behl

Dear Laura,
Happy reading and all
the best to you!

Robi Behl

NDSU NORTH DAKOTA STATE
UNIVERSITY PRESS

Fargo, North Dakota

NDSU NORTH DAKOTA STATE UNIVERSITY PRESS

North Dakota State University Press
Dept. 2360, P.O. Box 6050, Fargo, ND 58108-6050
www.ndsupress.org

First Edition
First Printing

Library of Congress Control Number: 2020934552
ISBN: 978-1-946163-17-2 (paperback)
ISBN: 978-1-946163-45-5 (hardcover)

Cover design by Jamie Trosen
Interior design by Deb Tanner

The publication of *Price Per Barrel: The Human Cost of Extraction* is made possible by the generous support of donors to the NDSU Press Fund and the NDSU Press Endowment Fund, and other contributors to NDSU Press.

David Bertolini, Director
Suzzanne Kelley, Publisher
Zachary Vietz, Graduate Publicity Assistant in Publishing
Oliver West Sime, Graduate Editorial Assistant in Publishing
Grace Boysen, Alexis Melby, Kalley Miller: Editorial Interns

Book Team for *Price Per Barrel: The Human Cost of Extraction*
Laura Ellen Brandjord, Luke Hauge, Alexis Melby, Corrine Redding

Printed in in the United States of America

Publisher's Cataloging-In-Publication Data
(Prepared by The Donohue Group, Inc.)

Names: Behl, Robin Lynn, author.
Title: Price per barrel : the human cost of extraction / by Robin Lynn Behl.
Description: First edition. | Fargo, North Dakota : North Dakota State University Press, [2021]
Identifiers: ISBN 9781946163172 (paperback) | ISBN 9781946163455 (hardcover)
Subjects: LCSH: Behl, Robin Lynn. | First responders--United States--Biography. | First responders--Mental health. | Oil fields--Social aspects--United States. | Mines and mineral resources--Social aspects--United States. | Migration, Internal--Social aspects--United States. | LCGFT: Autobiographies. | BISAC: BIOGRAPHY & AUTOBIOGRAPHY / Personal Memoirs. | MEDICAL / Allied Health Services / Emergency Medical Services. | TRAVEL / United States / General.
Classification: LCC HV551.3 .B44 2021 (print) | LCC HV551.3 (ebook) | DDC 363.3480973--dc23

This book is dedicated to the memory of
John Ivan Sutter.
8/21/1975 – 2/5/2010

Contents

Introduction

It was in the province of Newfoundland that I first heard about Fermont, Quebec. I was living in Maine, working as a physician assistant with a cardiology group. The job of practicing medicine in that mid-sized hospital environment was a mix of abject terror and soul-crushing boredom. Experiencing it as a type A woman in a type A man's environment was disappointingly familiar. After thirteen life-shaping years as a first responder—initially as a firefighter, then as an EMT-Basic, then a dispatcher, and a paramedic—I had hoped that pursuing a master's degree in medicine might elevate me to a work environment that was safer and more sophisticated. I'd hoped it would be equally altruistically motivated, but less crude and less disappointing. It was neither.

As a young firefighter in college, writing a paper for a freshman English class, I came across a book that would subtly alter the course along which the ship of my life was sailing. It was called *On Fire*, and the author, Larry Brown, was a firefighter in Oxford, Mississippi. Standing among the stacks in the New Mexico State University library, back in the days of card catalogues and computer labs, years before I would buy a cell phone or a laptop, I found myself distracted by his words.

At ten o'clock that night, I'd gone to that shelf to find the book that was catalogued next to his. But the title and the cover art grabbed my sleep-deprived attention. I plucked it from the shelf and opened it. After the first three chapters, I sat down on the rolling foot stool. Then eventually, I sat on the carpeted floor with my back against the stacks. I closed the back cover sometime after midnight, my submission deadline long forgotten. Mr. Brown was speaking a language I understood, in the most literal sense. He was speaking directly to me, with a timbre and a meter that resonated deeply with me. He was describing a job that I was just coming to know as the calling of my life.

Every page had some bit of description about the tools or about the firehouse that was so accurate and so familiar that I could smell the diesel exhaust as I read it. Every chapter reflected some moment I had already lived. And those that I would come to live. It was so vivid that I could smell the iron of spilled blood.

Back then, a quarter of a century ago, Larry and I diverged on one crucial point. He didn't want to do the job anymore. "I love being off duty," he wrote.

I can still remember that opening line of one of the early chapters. He talked about how on his day off he was so happy that he wanted to lie down in his carport and kick and scream with joy. Sitting amongst those moldy books at the tender age of eighteen, I couldn't identify with that feeling at all. I loved every second of the work. And I wanted nothing more than to do it as a career, for a lifetime. It was something I wanted so badly. More than marriage. More than children. More than a house or a car or an education.

I wanted to don that bunker jacket and polish those boots and key up that radio more than I wanted to breathe. It wasn't just the calls and the work, the humping hose and cutting up cars. I loved the sound of my duty boots as I walked across the apparatus bay. I loved the exhilaration of cruising through red lights with sirens blaring. I loved the relief in the eyes of bystanders when we showed up on a scene. It felt cinematic to me, even in the mundane, especially in the bizarre. It was the setting of what would become an uncommon life, a wonderful life.

In time, I learned not only to understand and appreciate the way Captain Brown savored his off-time, but also to embody it. There were days, deep in the throes of three jobs and double-overtime, that a day off could make me weep, actually weep, with joy. Eventually I learned, as he did, that the hardest part of the job is not the calls. It's not the patients. Nor the trauma. It's the other men and women in the firehouse. And the rule-makers outside it.

Human relationships are hard. In the pressure cooker of high-intensity work, they are harder. And for anyone outnumbered by demographic or gender, they are hardest yet. Larry Brown knew that. That's what motivated him to write. He motivated me to write. And to drive. And to ask questions. And eventually, to write this book. It is armament against my own insanity. It is intended to be instructional for municipal leaders, extractive industry executives, and members of public safety chains of command.

Above being instructive, I hope that *Price Per Barrel* is comfort to my brothers and sisters in blue, in brown, in white, and in arms to know that they are not alone in their doubts, nor in their shivers. I hope they know through this illustration, this celebration of their labor, that they and their work are valued.

Though I've been off duty entirely for a couple of years, I'm always thinking of them, the on-duty crews. Every windy, rainy day. Every dark, snowy night. I tuck into the warmth and security of my bed each night, knowing that nothing is likely to call me out of it. I think of them . . . and wish them well. Every holiday, I think of their families.

The work we do is noble when it's done nobly by noble people. Other than that, it's just work. People in uniform are not heroes. They are blue-collar laborers who are trained and equipped to do a specific job. And they're mostly good people. But there are the worst among us, who tarnish the sheen off a badge we've all worked so hard to polish. When a young firefighter realizes that men in blue shirts are just men—fallible, imperfect, and often egotistic—it can be disheartening. Women too. An asshole in a blue shirt is still an asshole, she's just wearing a blue shirt.

It was the noble crowd, in every department, that drew me to and kept me in the job, often believing in me when no one else did. Giving me a chance when no one else would. But there were also the jerks, the abusers, and the liars, who added weight to the burden we already collectively carried.

In leaving emergency medicine for white-coat medicine, I nursed a fantasy that it would be different. It wasn't.

So, I started to drive. Every chance I got, I drove somewhere, anywhere. And that's how I found myself in Newfoundland in the lingering winter of late April. I'd driven up from southern Maine and taken the ferry to Sydney, Nova Scotia, to Port aux Basques, Newfoundland. I slept fitfully on a ferry the size of a cruise ship, tossed like a toy in the tides of the Cabot Strait. Then I took an older boat from Newfoundland to mainland Labrador. We broke ice off the coast and it made the fishermen nervous. I drove a quarter of the way up the eastern stretch of the Trans-Labrador Highway and got snowed-in in Mary's Harbour.

With time to kill and nowhere to go, I befriended the plow man. He drove a tractor that threw snow up a thirty-foot wall, instead of pushing it with a shovel. We could barely converse, me in my American English, him in his Labradorean dialect. I rode with him on a plow the size of a Texas road-grader and watched him build up the barricade of snow that had been there since December and wouldn't melt until late June.

Because I couldn't get out of Mary's Harbour, I missed the ferry back to Newfoundland, the ferry back to Nova Scotia, and a day of work in the hospital. I was so happy about it that I lay down in the freshly-fallen April snow and kicked and screamed like Larry Brown.

When I was once again southbound under my own power, I tuned the radio to Canadian Broadcasting (CBC). I was all alone on a desolate stretch of highway. I had no food, but I had hot coffee. A story came on, and I had nothing but time to listen to it. It would turn out to be a story that would comfort me, connecting me to other humans in that far-flung desolation. It would feed me, in the curiosity of a new place, a new story. It would inspire me to drive, to write, to ask questions, and ultimately to put my stethoscope on a shelf for six months while I drove around North America.

The story on CBC that day was about a tiny iron-mining town in far northern Quebec, 760 miles north of Montreal and right on the border with Labrador. It's the kind of place that no one thinks of and no one goes to, unless they work there. The Arctic is replete with natural resources, but those resources are logistically complicated and very expensive to extract. Certain countries and certain companies are notorious for economic dumping: exploiting a community and a labor force, then abandoning them nearly overnight when the price of ore drops. The American West, the Arctic Circle, and parts of Africa and South America are littered with the detritus left behind by those players.

The town featured in that Canadian radio broadcast was conjured, designed, and built to combat that problem head-on, from the start. Fermont, Quebec, was to be the northern mining town of the future. As a social experiment, it worked.

It still works. While other communities in the wider geographic region have faltered, Fermont has persisted. Where the twenty-first-century pop-up towns in the Bakken Formation dealt with chaos and the loss of cultural memory, Fermont built a town that was orderly, mathematically functional, and aesthetically pleasing. Then the people grew a brand-new culture within its walls.

• • •

As my tires crunched along that barren stretch of Newfoundland highway, the woman on the radio crunched through the snow of Fermont, in her mukluks, to where her dog-sled team was waiting. In a sultry Quebecois French-accented English, she described how running her dogs was like a meditation for her. I was entranced, listening. When the radio program ended and my spell was broken, I found myself an hour closer to Port aux Basques and laden with questions.

I felt like there was a vital part of the story of the community that was missing from the record. I wanted to know about the people who had done the work that I had done. What was it like to care for people in such a remote wilderness? Was there a hospital there? Did women have babies there? Was there a fire department that could handle a structure fire without the benefit of any outside help? How were the sick and injured evacuated if the weather was too poor to fly? How often was the weather too poor to fly? I made it my mission to find out.

There was little documentation to be had online. And, like most Arctic towns, the people I phoned were not interested in talking to me until I showed up in person. On top of that, there was a language barrier. Ninety percent of the population of Fermont identifies French as their primary language and 70 percent are monolingual. My sophomore French is suitable for finding a bathroom or ordering a meal, but certainly not adequate for an investigative interview. So, I realized, I had to go there. I had to see it for myself.

In the span of time that it took me to plan my trip and raise the money to take it, I developed a curiosity for other places, other towns in which my work environment would be dramatically different from the one I was in. For six months, I planned an epic road trip, twenty-six thousand miles. I was to start in Maine and head first to Fermont, Quebec. I'd be heading north along the opposite side of the Trans-Labrador Highway from the chunk that had serendipitously stranded me an extra day. The driving would be difficult and dangerous.

From Fermont, I'd drop down into Upstate New York and work my way west, through Pennsylvania, Indiana, Minnesota, and over to North Dakota. I wanted to know how my colleagues were coping with the madness that was new oil development in the Bakken.

The trip, as such things do, morphed into something completely different from what I'd expected. Along the way, I learned to follow my nose instead of following the map. To listen to the stories instead of trying to tell the one I thought I knew.

The journey was put on hold several times while I went back to do the work that paid the bills. In that time, my subjects matured. Their situations changed. Booms ended and were reborn nearby. It became a real-time illustration of the very premise of this book. In writing about the people doing the hard work of caring for others in a changing world, I myself was changed.

There are some things that are universal to these places. Chiefly, that public servants, once called to duty, will refuse to abandon their posts. Even when their town changes completely, when their call volume quadruples, when the nature of the calls they're running changes along with the demographics, they stay. Secondly, post-traumatic stress disorder (PTSD) in public safety workers is real, contagious, and deadly. It is also treatable and modestly preventable with the right planning, the right support, and the right communication. Last, booms and busts will never go away. They've been a part of our country since the earliest days of the colonies and are a direct result of that colonization. Our modern world depends on the things that we mine and grow and catch, for better or for worse. And we will always come together in communities, for both sustenance and entertainment.

The housing market, the price of oil, and the need for speed have nothing to do with the cops and the medics and the fire-fighters. They're present no matter what: in Buckeye, Arizona, when the housing market crashes; in Watford City, North Dakota, when oil skyrockets; and at the Indy 500 on race day.

Sometimes things don't work out the way we thought they would. In all those miles on the road, I never actually made it to Fermont. I was turned away at the Canadian border on Thanksgiving Day. But, eventually, my desire to see it could not be stayed. So, I raised money again, took time off again, and hopped on a De Havilland Dash 8 in the middle of a snow squall. Setting foot in Fermont, four years late, it all clicked. I remembered why I'd wanted to come in the first place. I remembered why the story of it had struck me so deeply.

Even after all that time on the road, all the intervening years, all the incredible people I'd met, the public servants of Fermont still melted my heart. In the darkness of the arctic winter, they were like candles on painted windowsills. Against the frigid wind, they were a buttress. In giving breath to their stories, they warmed me. Caretakers always do. It is to them, not just in Quebec, but at every latitude, not just in the fire department, but in every uniform, that I owe this book and this life that I lead. In knowing them, I know I'm not alone. Even if there's no one else around.

Watford 4 Life

Revisiting the North Dakota oil fields after the
Bakken boom has ended
Watford City, North Dakota. Summer.

This place smells like fresh paint and stale farts.

I walk into my hotel, my summer flip-flops making the loudest noise in the empty hallway. It's supposed to be an upgrade from the man camp I stayed in when I was here last. That was four years ago. I just left a new beer pub that also smells of fresh paint, alongside new layers of hamburger grease. There, some kid had told me he was going to have "Watford for Life" tattooed on his body to memorialize his time here.

He was being sarcastic. But he's been here for six years. That's a long time in this environment. It's long enough to have seen the changes. We devolved into a frank and descriptive discussion of the anatomic choice for the geographic placement of his new tattoo. We decided on the "taint," that little piece of skin between the anus and the testicles.

From there, our conversation turned to mushrooms. He forages for them back home in Vermont. On his phone, he showed me pictures of fungi, both the culinary and the psychotropic. He lamented over missing morel season and about how he'd yet to find a hen of the woods. I asked him if he'd turn up his nose at a pedestrian white button mushroom. He took a slow sip of foamy beer and soberly replied, "All mushrooms matter."

I almost spit the newly fermented North Dakota beer out of my nose, but I managed to rein it in and swallow it. The beer smelled like farts too. My man camp, back then, didn't smell. It was too cold for any scent whatsoever. There wasn't even the rotten-egg smell of natural gas then. There still isn't now. That upsets me, because I know it means they're just flaring it off instead of capturing it.

Last time I was in Watford City, it was the depth of winter and the height of the Bakken madness. I found it so unsettling and kinetic that I still vibrate when I talk about it, four years later. With the price of oil so low right now that they're barely running the pumpjacks and doing virtually no new drilling, this place is positively placid. It shocks me at first as I drive into town, disoriented by the green grass where before there was dirty snow, and by the crisp, open pavement where before there were lines of semitrucks wearing deep grooves into two-lane farm roads.

Before, there were so many drilling rigs that from any high point, I could see at least five. Now, I can't find even one. Before, this place hummed, churned, quivered with the constant drilling, constant road grading, constant shouting and fighting. There was the swinging of fists and the swinging of dicks and the slinging of hot cash. There was coke and meth and Red Bull. There was Fireball whiskey, nearly freezing in the shot glass in the thirty-below. I could only stay outside for ten minutes without my hands aching, only stay in the bar for ten seconds without someone grabbing my ass, and only stay in town for three days before I started to turn.

It was only after leaving that it would dawn on me just how fucked up that place was, unlike anything I'd ever known, even having grown up in the oil patch, even having been on the North Slope of Alaska. It was terrifying and positively exhilarating. The

Bakken hit me on some base level that made me hungry and made me horny. This was an eat or be eaten, fuck or get fucked kind of town and it shocks me now that I miss it, a little bit.

As I pull in, marveling at the new concrete roads and the new shiny buildings, I start driving in a widening circle around town. My mouth hangs open like my July car windows, windows I wouldn't have dreamed of cracking in February of 2013. I can't get over what I'm seeing . . . and hearing. Something is strikingly different, and it takes me a minute to figure it out. Then it comes out of my mouth, aloud, to my windshield, a revelation. "There are women here."

That's what the thing is. The man camps are almost all gone. There are new ranks of apartment buildings, new paint on old houses, and new mansions on the periphery. And there are flowers. "There are fucking flowers!"

Flowers in window boxes, flowers on balconies, flowers lining driveways and flanking front doorways. Hanging flowerpots, stacked flowerpots, claw-foot tubs full of blossoms. Dudes in man camps don't plant flowers. The transient crews that come in for their two-week hitch barely clean the mud off their boots before they go into the supermarket, much less maintain a homestead.

There are women here now. Families. Bicycles and strollers and screaming kids on the playground. There are minivans and Honda Civics and mailboxes with last names on them. And there is way, way more town than there used to be. I stop on a hill where, before, I'd frozen my fingers off trying to take photographs of the mass and the chaos of a new drill site with its crew of twenty-five. Now, there's just the solitary pumpjack. It has a couple of holding tanks, and green grass with rolls of yellow hay that are baled and waiting for transport. Next to it is an entire new neighborhood, with dozens of four-story apartment buildings, paved streets, teenagers walking in the sun, and open garages full of the stuff of suburban American life.

It's weird. The more I drive, the weirder it gets. I drive past the old hospital, a tiny 1950s red-brick building that was supposed to transition into a new hospital four years ago, and I am disappointed to see that it's still occupied. Four years ago, they were supposed to be weeks away from breaking ground on the new joint.

"Figures," I say pessimistically as I drive past. Promises made in the oil field are rarely kept. But a couple blocks away, I'm surprised again. "Holy shit!" I say to no one.

The new hospital jumps off the prairie at me, twenty times larger than the old one, all glass and Tyvek, weeks away from completion. I round it, and up on the hill is another new set of houses. In front of one house, there's a Watford City Police Department SUV with "K-9 Unit" stenciled on the windows. I know who lives there. It's the young, green police chief and his sergeant wife, who were just "expecting" a police puppy when I was here. I know he's not the chief anymore. The county finally hired some grizzly old veteran from another department to relieve the twenty-eight-year-old who'd stepped up to fill some really heavy temporary shoes.

Now they've got this big house on the hill and a working dog with four years of experience. "Good for you, Jesse," I say as I turn around in their driveway. I hope he and his wife are still together, still happy, still healthy . . . still alive.

Places like this have a way of killing people. A way of killing marriages and clogging arteries and graying hairs. Part of me wants to knock on the door, see how things are going. And part of me can't bear it. I don't wanna know. There's a new mayor. I don't wanna know him either. He's a different generation of Watford. He doesn't interest me. The hard work was done before he got here. He's just like the women with their strollers and their well-stocked grocery store.

This is the easy part. The horror's already been gone through. And all those people on the front lines, the firefighters, the medics, the cops, the dispatchers, with their weathered skin and their worn souls, have passed the torch to the fresh faces of the next thirty years of public service. I'm wistful for this place, which is odd, because it's something, some place, I never had. I didn't live here. I didn't work here. But I took an interest in the people who were in the midst of caring for people in the midst of the madness that descended over these grasslands.

I cared about them. They were tasked with something beyond them and they rose to it. And now, all those assholes they labored to save, all those people for whom they risked their lives and their coronaries, they're all gone. They're back to Louisiana or Texas or Oklahoma or Venezuela. But they changed my friends, my brothers-in-arms, forever, just like those drilling rigs changed the literal topography here. And there's no changing back.

I wax nostalgic as I drive to the edge of town, south, to my old man camp. It was a tiny, terrible, temporary place that gave me a brief respite from the brutal cold, the driving snow, and the inexorable wind. The walls sheltered me from frostbite and the lock on the door sheltered me from all the swinging dicks. The view is different now. My old two-lane road dead-ends into a raised embankment, thirty feet high and supporting a new four-lane divided highway that pushes right to the threshold of my little old trailer. Behind it, where my solitary window had given onto a surreal and bucolic set of rolling hills, reminiscent of a Microsoft screensaver and dotted with white-tailed deer, now there are three enormous white holding tanks and a garbage dump.

The people in the man camp now are the bottom of the working barrel, too transient or too criminal for a home loan. And here's where it hits me that all that shit is still here, it's just covered in lipstick and flowers now. There's still meth. There's still coke. There's still the guy in the pub wanting to fuck. There are still hundreds and hundreds of flares wasting precious natural gas up into the still-lit nighttime sky. There's still the greed and the competition and the cover-up and the best and worst of us. There are still the heroes and the villains. But now, they look just like every-one else and everywhere else. There's no story here anymore. As sparkly as everything is now, it's just another oil town that built a lot of stuff during the boom that will rust and crumble in the downturn like all the others.

Last time, this place made me want to have sex. Now, it just makes me want to leave. Because even though it's covered in fresh paint, it still smells like stale farts.

Black Thursday

Turned away at a Canadian checkpoint on Thanksgiving Day
Jackman, Maine. Winter.

"Your dog just peed on my sleeping bag," I say, facing blank stares. "You realize that could kill me tonight?" Polite, but still silent, the Canadian customs agents are unmoved, as unmoved as they are when I explain why I want my perfectly legal, well-researched, and safely locked shotgun at my side. I am planning to sleep along the Trans-Labrador Highway, in early winter, alone.

I stand in the rapidly approaching November dusk, while the biting Canadian air drives the icy snow into our faces. I am standing next to Frankie, my Nissan Frontier, in which I intend to live the next six months, in which I intend to circumnavigate the United States. It is the truck I've studiously chosen and meticulously outfitted to take me into the frozen far north of Canada. It is the truck that is going to be my only defense against the wind and the bears and the wolves. Frankie, along with my Mossberg 20-gauge youth model smoothbore 3-in-1 shotgun. I've meticulously researched that weapon as well, since I knew I'd be headed across the frontier on my way to Fermont, Quebec, up on the Labrador border. The Trans-Labrador Highway is one of the most remote and least utilized routes in North America. It's a lonely,

lonely road. But I'm ready for it. It isn't the first lonely road I'll have driven. And I've been planning it for months. Yet here I am, foiled and freezing, my pleas falling on stoic, polite faces.

I could have just lied. When the customs agent, cleanly shaven, late fifties, sexy in that little arrogant way that both men in uniform and French-Canadian men can be, asked me if I had anything to declare, I could have said no. I'd be sixty miles into the spruce woods by now if I had. But being a good girl by training, I'd told the truth and now my naughty nature was coming out in full force.

I tell him I am heading to Fermont and that I am carrying a shotgun, and I hand him my pre-filled declaration form, my US firearms registration, the Canadian firearm fee, and a printout of the State Department's website that proves my weapon is permissible in Canada. His polite, arrogant smile turns to a polite, arrogant frown as he takes my papers and my passport. He spends some time looking at my profile in the computer, and then sticks his head out of the window of his booth, fat white flakes peppering his hat badge. "Pull there, madame." He points to a covered parking area. He disappears inside with my money and my passport.

"Fuck," I grunt, steeling myself for what's coming. These guys, with sidearms instead of AKs and parkas instead of green fatigues, are one-third as intimidating as the *federales* of Mexico on our southern border or as the Russian immigration man who threw me off a train in eastern Finland, but still, they can really foil my plans. I'm burning daylight and precious fuel idling here in Jackman, Maine, on Thanksgiving Day.

"I don't have time for this," I whisper through teeth plastered into a complacent and non-threatening smile. A band of ten of them wander out of their warm yellow-lit guard building. The only one with a rifle comes to my driver's door and holds it aside for me, patiently waiting while I gather my coat, my hat, and my gloves. "You may wait inside where it's warm if you wish."

"I'll be fine here for a few minutes," I say, donning my cap and flashing teeth. Without another word he shoulders his weapon, sits in the seat I've just vacated, and turns off my ignition. I suppress an eye roll. Here we go.

They descend on Frankie like grasshoppers on summer corn, turning him out and opening him up. All my carefully packed things, including my shotgun, come out of storage and onto the ten inches of newly fallen snow. A man I hadn't previously seen carries my locked shotgun case inside, out of view. Another carries the box of shells, stored separately, handling them like the makings of an atomic bomb. Out comes the extra ten gallons of gas, the two weeks of food, the fire starters, matches, and candles. Out comes the CB radio and the maps and the two fully-mounted studded snow tires, my spares. Out comes the jack and the tire wrench and the orange triangles and the traffic flares. Out comes my bedding and my bed and all my clothes. They open my cargo trunk and pull out my panties, my bras, my high heels, and my extra pair of snow boots.

A young man pulls out my rolled-up sleeping bag, moving to set it on the ground. He catches my watchful eye and stops an inch above the snow, choosing instead to let it rest in one of the spare tires they'd pulled out from under Frankie's matching camper shell. I nod my thanks to his consideration. He seems to be the only one who understands that this truck and everything in it is my whole life. It is everything I, in my über-minimalist life, own. And I am at a literal crossroads, leaving behind a job, a paycheck, a warm house and warm friends, a social life, and a modest social standing. I'm leaving it all, taking what I can cash out of my retirement and seduce out of my supporters, and heading off to write something about some place none of these guys around me knows about.

Many months ago, a lonely voice on the radio had brought me the story of Fermont and I'd been enraptured. It had been an intimate slice of humanity that made me warm on those barren, frozen roads. I'd committed then, to learning more about those people. In the intervening year, I'd dreamt of it, studied it, looked at maps, planned routes, raised funds, and brushed aside the snickers and the scorn of people who'd dismissed the idea.

And here, at the Border Patrol station in Jackman, these polite assholes are about to derail me. After they tear Frankie apart, they stand in a half-circle between us, between me and my truck, between me and what is now everything in the world I own. The sergeant, now with more snowflakes on his uniform hat, asks me why I need the shotgun.

"For protection. I'm going all the way to Fermont."

"Protection from what?"

Behind him, an outdoor television screen scrolls the pictures and names of one hundred twenty-five missing persons who've disappeared in Quebec over the past five years. Indigenous women especially disappear by the dozens in the North American Arctic every year. I let my gaze flicker toward the TV and then answer him directly.

"Bears . . . wolves . . . moose . . . people."

It's that last word that makes the ten of them, now swollen to a baker's dozen, laugh in that polite, arrogant, wide-stance way that law enforcement officers can.

"This is Canada. We're very safe here."

"Any of you ever driven to Fermont?" I look from one to the other, as they each shake their heads. I already knew their answer. It's a four-day drive from here.

"Have any of you ever been to Fermont at all?" More shaking heads.

"It's quite far," the sergeant says.

The dimming gray and the silent falling of snow are suddenly broken by a stream of hot, fragrant urine, sizzling as it melts some ice. We all look over to the French-Canadian German Shepherd who had sniffed all of Frankie and was now marking him as his own by peeing on one of the spare tires, the one on which my twenty-below-rated sleeping bag had been so thoughtfully perched by that young agent.

"Your dog just peed on my sleeping bag. You realize that could kill me tonight."

"Pack up your things and then come inside, madame."

And they leave me there, in the snow under the parking cover. I try my best to return all my things to their previously planned spaces, hefting both spare tires, one cold, the other slick and warm, back just inside the tailgate. I refasten their bungee cords, positioning them over the rear wheels where their weight will give me a bit more traction. I spread out my North Face bag, the one that's soaked with dog piss, the one that had kept me warm in Greenland and cozy in Alaska, so that it might dry before I have to climb into it tonight.

I join the whole dispatch of customs agents inside, peeling off my hat, my gloves, and my Canada Goose Arctic Expedition Series parka. They all go into the breakroom, and leave me with the sergeant who, despite my charm, my reason, my pleading, and my demanding, adamantly refuses to let me into Canada with my shotgun.

"Well, I can't just leave it here with you . . . Soooo . . . "

"You could take it back to Jackman and mail it home."

"It's Thanksgiving . . . "

A pause.

"You cannot come here."

Another pause.

I turn again to the television with the faces of the missing. I gesture. "I suppose it's best. I might never be seen again."

That's my bad girl coming out, but I have nothing to lose. I walk back out to my truck and drive it around to the American side, where the little flunky who'd tried to honor my property had taken my shotgun. He gives it to the US guy and taps his booney hat to me. I meet his gaze.

"I've never known anybody who's been to Fermont," he says quietly.

"Well," I said. "You can read all about it in my book. I'll get there someday."

"Bon voyage."

And in that frigid dusk of northern Maine, on a night when "normal" Americans are watching football with sleepy bellies of turkey and pie, I know he means it. It's so sweet that I forget that he and his friends took my money.

Cold Brew

The depth of winter and the height of the latest oil boom
Watford City, North Dakota. Deep winter.

It's 3 a.m., in the dead of winter, at the top of North Dakota. And it's cold. It's snowing. There's only the black of night, the white of the blowing snow, and the alien red reflecting off the clouds. This is the oil patch. And I've gone Bakken crazy.

We're all crazy here. The world is full of beaches and sunshine and warmth. But we're here. In the cold. There's no mystique to it, like there is in Alaska. There's no open ocean to it, like in South Texas. There's no glamour to it, like California. The only glamour in the Bakken tonight is the little, plastic, turquoise carnation the bartender has stuck in the acres of dark, curly, flowing hair on her head. It distracts my eye momentarily northward, from the acres and acres of brown-skinned cleavage pouring and bouncing out the top of her low-cut, black tank top.

Somewhere between the tits and the turquoise carnation lay her eyes. They are eyes that reveal a wisdom to work the angle God gave her, to empty the wallets of the drunken sailors at her feet.

These men, by the score, are not in the starched and pressed white of those who sail the seas. They're not even in the camouflage of those who defend our liberty. They are, instead, in the greasy, oil-covered, mud-splattered denim and canvas of their chase.

Digging, digging, driving, drilling. Not toward the thick black viscous oil forced skyward by thousands of gallons of pressurized saltwater. Not for the sweet stank of natural gas blowing and glowing red toward the empty night sky, where it lights the snow falling on roads worn to the bare dirt from which they were built. These men, covered in their own stank, chase green.

When they can pull their eyes from the breasts of the four women in town long enough to see it, they chase green. I can scarcely make out their scarcely intelligible words over the din. The din of diesel engines idling relentlessly through this godforsaken cold. The din of tires on ice-covered, frost-heaved blacktop. The din of the drilling and the flaring and the ceaseless ticking of snowflakes against glass.

This is not the healthy, fluffy snow of snowmen and snowball fights. This is malignant snow. The hard kind that stings your face and wets your gloves and slides its way down the back of your neck, shivering the length of your spine until it finds your soul and wraps its frozen blue hands around it. The kind that comes down not in big fluffy heaps but instead drives sideways, into your ears, into your eyes, your mouth, your breath, your very heart, until it, too, beats a drum so muffled and dead that not even the bats could hear it.

This is the Bakken, and it's not normal. Nowhere should look like this, with headlights from semitrucks lighting the 3 a.m. road like a snake of liquid fire burning across the National Grasslands. Nowhere so rural should have roads grooved so deeply that one can drive without steering for miles, even navigating the turns as if fixed to a rail. Nowhere should have so much testosterone and greed and madness, when before it was the breadbasket of the nation, the womb of life. There shouldn't be a flaming red sky. There should be stars and silence and a snow with less malevolence.

I hear a great sucking, a great suckling at the teat of our dependence on fuel, our gluttony of energy consumption, our egotistic and maniacal drinking from the bottomless cup of wealth and comfort. This place is not normal.

I figured I'd be able to find it by the smell. The Bakken oil fields of North Dakota are some of the richest, hottest, and highest producing shale sands ever discovered in North America. A child of the oil patch, I'm familiar with that rotten egg "smell of money." That ever-present reminder of the economic basis of my hometown. And I figured that would be the tip-off that I'd arrived.

Instead, driving west from Sioux Falls and north from Dickinson, the first things I noticed were the job postings. Billboards advertised truck-driving jobs and efficiency housing. Flyers taped on restaurant doors looked for cooks and servers and delivery drivers. Bathroom stalls became telephone directories for placement agencies and domestic abuse hotlines. Even the convenience store countertop, underneath my credit card slip, was emblazoned with employer want ads.

I figured, as I made my way north, I'd ease into it by seeing the big trucks and the industrial supply yards with acres of pipe and fittings, then finally the pumpjacks and tanks that are the meat and potatoes of oil extraction in our country.

It wasn't that gentle. No sooner had my attention been diverted by the canyons of Theodore Roosevelt National Park, carved by the Little Missouri River, than I was up and out and firmly in it. In the Bakken.

Maybe it doesn't look abnormal to those who have no frame of reference for it, but it looks abnormal to me, the oil patch kid. The stuff is the same: tan or green painted pumpjacks rocking placidly, marking time in the blowing snow. Batteries of storage tanks patiently waiting for the truck to come relieve them of their liquid burden. Drilling rigs sparkling in the dusk, droning of progress and development.

Each of those, singly, is part of the Rolodex of my mind. What's not normal is the sheer number, the number of everything. The first active drilling site is visible as soon as I crest the hills at the edge of the national park. And everywhere I look on the horizon is another, and another, and another. Growing up, if after driving for an hour I'd seen two new sites being drilled, I knew the economy was looking up. Here, from one hilltop, I see five rigs.

On each well, instead of a solo pumpjack, they're all in pairs. I had rarely ever seen that before. Now, every well has at least two, often three, sometimes even four of those One-Eyed-Jacks sucking perpetually from the earth. And they're all new. The wellheads, the tanks, there's not an ounce of rust marring their shiny new paint. Everything gleams and sparkles, foreshadowing nothing of the industrial decay that will inevitably come to this place, as it has to my hometown.

Many of the oil field office buildings here have the same 1980s façade that I'm familiar with, yet they sit on new concrete pads with young shrubbery around them. It's as if, in their hurry to literally tap into this market, these companies dusted off some blueprints in some attic in West Texas and used them to nail together what they could and get to drilling.

Then there are the trucks, hundreds of them. Eighteen wheels of mud and ice racing around the clock, wearing grooves in the two-lane blacktop. Sixty-five percent of the traffic on these little farm roads is big rig traffic.

The limited pipeline infrastructure and single in-state refinery can't possibly keep up with demand here, so everything moves by truck and by train. There is earth-moving equipment for building roads and clearing pads. There are water trucks providing fracking fluid and propane trucks supplying all the temporary housing units.

Then there are the flares. A by-product of hydraulic fracturing is natural gas, along with propane and butane and C5. And without a pipeline to harness those gasses, there's no cost-effective, logistically smooth way to utilize it. So instead, it's all combusted through a system of flares that dot the earth like candles on a giant birthday cake. So many flares that the nighttime sky is never dark. It dances like a summer thunderhead or a Hollywood movie premiere.

Approaching a flare, I'm surprised by how much noise it makes, like a jet engine. Millions of BTUs are literally going up in smoke, so much so that one expects the January night to be hot instead of the negative twenty degrees that makes me shiver inside my heated truck. The flares can, literally, be seen from space, they are so many.

The only thing more numerous than the flares and the trucks, are the man camps. Man camps are acres and acres of temporary housing units strewn across the grassland to house the mostly fly-in/fly-out oil field workers, the vast majority of whom are men. There are some man camps that are well organized, gated, guarded, and managed by companies who provide such workforce housing all over the world. There are others that are nothing more than a pack of campers and garden sheds sprouting out of gas station parking lots, none of them rated for a North Dakota winter.

Each of them adds to the hazard burden of this place. It makes me cringe for the firefighters, volunteers all. So much lightweight construction packed so closely, supplied with propane, and occupied by cigarette smokers in a region of the country often boasting 30-mph winds, looks to me like a conflagration waiting to happen. One tornado here and hundreds of people will die. A fast moving prairie fire will lead to evacuation bottlenecks. A little too little hand washing and this becomes a pandemic petri dish. And so many of the living quarters are so close to the jobsites that an explosion or leak or sustained fire is going to impact a lot more people than just the forty guys on the drilling rig itself.

The sheer number of vehicles on the road, lots of them carrying hazardous materials, have made this county, McKenzie

County, the worst in the state for traffic fatalities, almost the worst in the nation. There's just so much opportunity for human error. Many drivers are fatigued here. Freelance truck drivers are paid by the load, not by the hour, which is why the gas station shelves are filled to the brim with case after case of Monster and Red Bull and Rockstar and 5-hour Energy and Mountain Dew Code Red. Coffee seems an afterthought here.

There is no official start to the workday in the Bakken. That day started five years ago and hasn't ended since. Highway 85 winds like an electric snake through the once-peaceful hayfields, lit by the headlights of a hundred tractor-trailers. And it takes me right up to Main Street and downtown Watford City, North Dakota, the epicenter of the Bakken boom.

Watford City was an agricultural town of one thousand people that has seen a tenfold increase in population, up to ten thousand at last, best count, and climbing. There was, and is, no way for the city leaders to forecast growth accurately. Every projection has been blown out of the water in six months. Until this past July, there wasn't even a full-scale grocery store here. Now, Cash Wise Foods is doing its own booming business. And they're not the only ones. The local hospital is serving a population of ten thousand out of a building designed for a town of fifteen hundred.

Everywhere, there is new construction: restaurants, laundromats, and four-story hotels filling some of the most expensive rooms in the country. New apartment complexes and rows of condos and entirely new neighborhoods are bristling out of the fields like springtime growth. All of this, with no full-time building inspector, no full-time fire inspector, and no mapping or platting staff. All of this, with a totally volunteer fire department, no ladder truck, and a fire chief whose full-time job is with the United States Forest Service, not with Watford City. All this with a small, twelve-bed hospital that hasn't changed much in the last fifty years. It's frighteningly inadequate.

The hospital, along with all the other public safety and healthcare agencies in the region, is trying to get ahead of the game again, by breaking ground on a new complex as soon as the earth thaws this spring. McKenzie County Healthcare Systems is recruiting providers from major metro areas and rural facilities alike who want the challenge of having to know a little bit about a lot of things and a lot about a few things.

Being a doctor or a mid-level provider here means that you get to shape and build your own practice but also that you are a family doc, a pediatrician, an obstetrician, an emergency room doctor, a pharmacist, a psychiatrist, and an occupational health guru. It's certainly not for the faint of heart or the slow of feet.

The biggest challenge to recruitment, according to Chief Operating Officer Mike Curtis, has been housing. It's hard to get a seasoned provider to relocate their family if there's nowhere to live. So the hospital, just like the city, is now in the real estate business, buying houses and apartments in which they can place new, incoming staff.

The same challenges and the same adrenaline face the small cadre of six full-time and part-time paramedics holding the life of McKenzie County, the second largest county in the nation, in their hands. The McKenzie County Ambulance Service's call volume has more than quintupled since the boom started, and with the combination of long response distances (up to seventy miles or more) and limited specialty care locally, helicopter transports have gone up from an average of six per year to ninety-five in 2013 alone, according to Director Kerry Krikava.

The ambulance service has become so busy that they, and local law enforcement, are now dispatched by State Radio in Bismarck. And it's not simply the volume of calls increasing, but also the nature of injuries and illnesses changing. There are more violent assaults, more drug- and alcohol-related injuries, more domestic violence calls, and a higher incidence of mental health emergencies than what previously constituted the typical calls here.

That's why the EMTs are now wearing bulletproof vests and the Watford City Police or McKenzie County Sheriff co-respond on all EMS calls. There has been an increase in 911 response at night, both due to higher numbers of customers in the local watering holes and the 24/7 nature of oil field work. For a group of responders that either volunteer or work EMS part-time, that sleep disruption takes a toll on their bodies, their families, and their full-time employment.

It's also hard on the rigs. Each ambulance would go through a windshield a week if they replaced every crack and chip. As it stands, it's hard enough to get a service team to Watford City to do the replacements, so only the most visually impairing windshields get fixed. The washboard roads just about rattle the boxes off the back of the ambulance and the tires get quickly shredded by the gravel. There's very little shoulder space for truck traffic to yield the right-of-way, further hampering response, and it can take up to five minutes for a vehicle with lights and sirens to get through the traffic light in the center of town.

Despite all that, the salty medics who live for such challenges are equipped with a broad scope of practice, liberal off-line medical control, and enough call variety to maintain a very high skill level. And according to Fire Chief Oscar Knudtson, all the emergency response agencies "play well together" in this frenetic sandbox.

Police officers and sheriff's deputies here are getting the equivalent of five years of experience in about half the time, according to Police Chief Jesse Wellen. And they're handling everything from methamphetamine and cocaine use by workers trying to stay awake, to strange animal-control issues with folks bringing exotic pets from all over the country, to home invasions, to improper disposal of radioactive materials at the local landfill. They are process serving and extraditing prisoners and deporting undocumented workers. They are facing language barriers and homelessness and impaired drivers, sometimes pursuing vehicles for over an hour with lights and sirens.

The age range of officers here varies from a young local police force, where the oldest officer is twenty-nine and the chief is twenty-eight, to the seasoned sheriff who has worn his uniform here for thirty-four years. With only fifteen deputies and ten municipal police officers, the agencies rely on each other and on surrounding federal agencies such as US Border Patrol; the Bureau of Alcohol, Tobacco, Firearms and Explosives; the Drug Task Force; and the North Dakota State Police for backup.

Each agency has had a quadrupling of call volume, without a quadrupling of qualified applicants for open positions. Housing cost and unavailability, the weather, and the long shifts make it difficult to recruit experienced, academy-trained officers who are both fully informed about what they're getting into and fully clean on background checks. Which means those officers who are already here, just like their other public safety counterparts, have risen far above and beyond the call of duty in caring for the town.

Sheriff John Fulwider's chest visibly swells with pride when he speaks of the dedication and honor with which his deputies do the job. The sheriff has been on the job far long enough to retire, but having raised his family in Watford City, he feels such an overwhelming sense of responsibility to this place that he can't bear to leave it just yet. That means he's still on the road, every day, doing traffic stops. He's awakened, every night without fail, for some major incident. His eyes, having seen so much in thirty-four years of police work, turn misty when he confides that he'd rather not see his grandchildren than have his family travel such dangerous roads to visit the place they've always called home. Sheriff Fulwider was here for the first boom in the 1980s, which he describes as much less frenetic, without man camps, and with more families instead of single men.

He's empathetic to the scores of people from this town, especially those who don't own the mineral rights to their land, who've had their entire peaceful way of life interrupted. They can no longer afford groceries. They don't feel safe on the roads, especially given the fact that if you're in a crash where your auto glass gets broken, the most serious threat to your life is hypothermia. Some of them are simply choosing to leave.

The ones who've stayed, just like the firefighters, EMTs, dispatchers, and law enforcement officers who serve them, are still, somehow, some of the nicest, most hospitable, generous, and trusting people on the planet. They've been able to retain their classic midwestern hospitality. And the folks in uniform here are the epitome of what we think the uniform should be: dedicated, professional, humble, concerned, and absolutely passionate about the work they do.

Having grown up in the oil field, having worked with mostly men my entire life, and having traveled the entirety of the United States and Canada alone, I'd never felt as unsafe as the day I drove into Watford City. By the time I left, having met the local public safety and healthcare team, I'd never felt so reassured of help, so renewed of faith in the goodness of people, or so proud of my brothers and sisters in uniform. But the Bakken, just like any other oil field, is a tense and overwhelming place to live when the price of oil is up. I didn't fully realize that until after I left. Once I had a chance to be away from it for a few days and analyze my own behavioral reactions to the place, I felt at once silly and primal. I realized I had been, in a word, horny.

Three days seems to be my tolerance of the place. I don't have the figures, but the place is more than predominantly or primarily men. It's profoundly men. I can hear it in the way the pickup trucks tear out of the parking lot like the end of a high school football game. I can taste it in the deep-fried, salted, alcoholic diet devoid of vitamins but plentiful in calories. I can see it in the unshaven faces and the coarse fabrics and the glassy, animalistic stares. I can smell it. Oh my lord can I smell it. It's sweat and salt. It's soap and cologne. It's masculinity and pheromones.

And I can feel it. I feel the heat off the shoulders lined up on either side of mine. I feel it in the movement of the crowd and the shaking of the ground from a million rubber tires. I feel someone standing too close behind me. I feel his breath on my face when he talks to me. I feel hands touching. First my arm, maybe my back. They try the leg and I move it. They try my face and I dodge it. They try my neck and I swat it, grab it, scratch it, move toward it to disarm it. I feel what he's pressing against my leg and I know that it's time to ask for the tab.

All of them, all of that, it does something to me. Clearly it does something to the men, too. Last night, a nice young man told me straight-faced that after twenty-eight days on the job, working hard and sleep deprived, with no women around, that "any man here would rape a woman and if he tells you he wouldn't he's lying or gay." Last night, that didn't strike me as odd. It struck me as plausible. Last night, a fully dressed young man rubbed his penis on my fully dressed leg and it didn't strike me as odd. It struck me as predictable.

What strikes me as odd today is that I want to have sex. I don't want children. I don't want a husband. I don't even want to be around anyone right now. I don't need a provider or a caretaker or any of that Hallmark shit. This is something different.

It's not cognitive. It's deeper than that. Not love, simpler than that. Not conversation, shallower than that. Not random, too predictable for that. Not scary, too natural for that. Not embarrassing, too human for that. And not possible, because I got out of there, that fragrant, palpable, delectable, dreadful sea of hormones bathing the Bakken, just in time.

Morenci and the View of the End of the Earth

North America's largest copper mine
Morenci, Arizona. Spring.

People from here will tell you there's no better place to live in the world. People who are not from here can't understand why anyone would ever spend a life here. Morenci, Arizona, is not a city. It's not a town. Not even a village or a hamlet or a township. It is an unincorporated part of Greenlee County and it is classified as frontier. Still.

At first glance, you can say that Morenci is about copper. But it's more than that. It's the biggest copper mining operation in North America. But what that really means is that a little piece of Morenci goes into almost everybody's home in the developed world.

Copper is in everything tech. From the cell phones in our pockets to the computers on our desks to the pacemakers keeping us alive and the fire trucks dousing water on our copper-wired, copper-plumbed houses. Every air conditioner in a window, every coin in a pocket, and every holstered gun contains copper. There's almost a mile of it in a modern car. It helps a ship's hull resist corrosion and a doorknob resist bacteria. It makes music when it's combined with zinc and molded into a trumpet. It marks time in the toll of a billion bells. And it speeds the flow of information across semiconductor superhighways.

Copper took humankind from the stone age to the modern age to the technology age to the romantic resurrection of the Moscow Mule. We, all of us, exist with it, in its processed form, every day, often unaware of it. And with all that, it's beautiful. A coffered ceiling, a gabled roof, a hammered bar top, they all look better with a little Cu. It's long been lauded for its medicinal properties, and its malleability suits it for statuary.

Copper is concentrated in a few places in the world. Most of it is found in the mountainous western parts of North and South America, especially in Arizona, New Mexico, and Chile.

None of those places are heavily populated. All of them are rugged and arid with a Cauldron of Creation property to them. That cauldron image is reinforced by the shape of the open-pit mine, a mountain in reverse. It's a really big hole, surrounded by a mountain of man's work. Driving on Route 191 at the extreme eastern edge of Arizona, if you're unprepared for what you're about to see it can be disconcerting.

Unplanned travelers to Morenci are rare. So, few people are surprised to see the pit. There's no reason to go through Morenci except to go to Morenci. It's not on the way to anything. It's a "can't get there from here and why would you want to" kind of place. No one comes to Morenci for the food, or the arts, or the music, or the schools, or the architecture, or the shopping. They come to work.

That said, the road running north to south through Morenci will occasionally draw an outdoor enthusiast who has read somewhere that the drive encompasses four climate zones in a scant one hundred miles. Which is true. The old timers will tell you, "This is not the end of the earth, but you can see it from here."

I drive through the alpine mountains of fur and pine, through the high desert scrub of piñon and mesquite, past the agricultural basin of cotton and cattle, and find myself clinging to the edge of a slag mountain made by machines. I stand on the flat ridge looking down on the stepped plains, locked in their angle of repose, and feel like a giant compared with the trucks a couple thousand feet below, moving like insects in their busy enterprise. I look up at the wide open sky, six thousand feet closer to the sun than the beach, and I feel like an ant. I feel tiny, insignificant, tasked with some burden, yet toiling toward some large framework that I'm too small to see.

In one hour's drive, I go from late winter to early summer, passing quickly through spring. This is the land of things that slither and scamper, from desert rattlers to one of the world's most venomous scorpions. Other things here walk softly, with carefully placed hooves and roughened tongues that are calibrated for the desert flora.

Deer, antelope, cattle, elk, and the regal bighorn sheep live here. They migrate through and they try to outrun the bear and the mountain lion here. On the wing are eagles and turkeys and vultures and a thousand songbirds, with the red of the cardinal and the royal of the bluebird and the yellow of the meadowlark. This county, Greenlee County, is long and tall with woodpeckers and starlings and rivers that run in all four seasons. It's also young, moving earth. It compresses into folds and rifts of minerals that make a find, that make a strike, that make a town like Morenci. It's a town where fathers, sons, brothers, everyone worked their whole lives for the mine.

From away, you'd think they'd know better. You'd think they'd know better than to stay in some outpost molded after a million others, where life is nothing more than what you do for work. But, from within, you come to appreciate that Morenci has everything a town needs to be a town.

Precisely because everybody does the same work and lives in the same house, life becomes about other things. Here, more clearly than anywhere else, it's not possible to judge the people around you by their work in the mine, by their vehicle (a big white truck), or by their home (which is company owned). When the houses look the same and the trucks look the same and the work is the same, the only thing different is the human.

Because of its geographic isolation and its single industry, Morenci has become a fishbowl in which life is lived on the common stage. Everyone knows everything about everyone, even, or especially, if it's untrue. People here either love that or hate that, probably depending on the rumor currently being circulated about them. Half the children who grow up in Morenci run screaming from it. And half of those come running back because they miss the order and organization and clearly-defined structure of it. The world at large is much more chaotic than Morenci. Some of Morenci's kids are drawn toward the military, precisely because the orderly routine feels familiar to them.

Freeport-McMoRan (FMI), the mining company, owns more than 95 percent of the town. Every home, every road, every signpost, and nearly every business. There's one pub located perfectly between the mine and all the houses, on literally everyone's way home, which is privately owned. There are also a few things owned by the county, much of it in partnership with the mine. Everyone who works for the county knows that the mine is the best friend and the worst enemy. The mine is a tremendous economic generator. In fact, the existence of the town depends upon it. But it's so big that nothing else around can possibly compete with it.

When a company is your bartender, your healthcare provider, your law enforcement, and your entertainment, it is nearly your everything. It's parochial. We expect such an omnipresence from the military, for military families. But most of us, as civilians, are unaware that such a monopoly exists on so large a scale in the private sector.

That omnipresence itself raises the stakes considerably when there's talk of a merger or buyout. A change of the guard strikes abject fear into the hearts of miners enticed by steady work, enlisted by competitive pay, and entrenched by the arrow-straight trajectory of their careers and the walls of rock that could crumble across the escape road at the slightest quake.

Then there's the boom. What should be endless benefit and untold riches can also be completely disruptive. Morenci has had steady employment and has continuously mined copper for over one hundred years with the exception of a brief respite during the Great Depression and a mandated cooling-off period during the infamous labor strike of 1983, when the National Guard held the line between corporate supporters and union loyalists. That otherwise unbroken production won't stop anytime soon.

Morenci is a place of longevity. Though there have been high-dollar and low-dollar years in copper's lifespan, Morenci is still around because they haven't hit the bottom of the hole yet. The rising demand for copper, matched by a rising price, is due in large part to a swelling middle class in several emerging first world economies, especially China. More people than ever in Asia, Africa, and South America are able to afford cars and cell phones, both packed with Morenci hillside.

A few years ago, a new "big brother" became the father of the town and changed the game. All who lived and worked in Morenci, who'd established their lives there, grown their children there, and counted on the life-giving pulse of the mine, fretted about the possibilities of new ownership. On the front lines of watching that stress manifest itself is Dr. Fred Fox, the medical director of Morenci's clinic.

If it isn't grown, it's mined. Almost everything we use to live our lives is either sown in a field, grown in a grove, raised in the sea, cut with an axe, or dug from the ground. There are people doing the fishing and the chopping and the harvesting. Here in Morenci, they do the digging. In order to dig, they have to be healthy. In order to be healthy, they need adequate healthcare.

That's where the clinic comes in. Morenci, as an isolated, self-sufficient company town, has no hospital, anymore. The old hospital building where several generations of Morenci babies were born, and where tuberculosis lungs were dried in the center courtyard, now functions as a world-class clinic.

It's not fancy. Inside it looks like a Norman Rockwell painting of a WPA doctor's office. So much so, that I almost expect to see stainless steel hypodermic syringes and glass IV bottles and doctors walking around with cigarettes between their teeth. I find none of those things here, but I do find an enormous caribou rack hanging on the wall in Dr. Fox's office.

Dr. Fox was a long-time family doctor in Silver City, New Mexico, another mining town just over the New Mexico border and about a ninety-minute drive from Morenci. When he came to this clinic, he brought some of his fellow providers with him and went on to recruit and retain a small corps of professional, empathetic, and extremely dedicated physicians, nurses, and physician assistants.

With only nine practitioners providing 24/7, 365 healthcare coverage, there are lots of opportunities to go way above and beyond the standard call of duty. This clinic is everything to everybody, serving all comers without regard for ability to pay and treating all stages of life from birth and before to death and beyond. It's family practice and urgent care and emergency medical services and occupational health and industrial response and coroner services all rolled into one.

For the nursing staff, all local, they never encounter a patient they don't know. For the providers, they're always treating one of their own. And for the paramedics, there are few remaining houses in town that they've never been inside. That's a level of intimacy with a community that few practices ever know these days, and it requires a sensitivity and humility that is unparalleled in the profession. It also requires every provider to be capable of a broad range of skills.

More than once, Dr. Fox has encountered a car that rolled off the road and down the steep embankment on his way home, joining his mine rescue team in hoisting victims up the hillside. He's gathered epidemiological information with the local health department, this place being perfect for statistics in its isolation. He's published research on scorpion envenomation and monoclonal antibody antivenin administration in children. He's the only one in the country to give this new serum, developed at the University of Arizona in Tucson, trialed at twenty-one southwestern hospitals and the Morenci clinic, to a twenty-four-day-old infant stung by a scorpion that dropped off the ceiling and into his crib.

He's seen his research come to significantly impact scorpion victims, making it possible to treat and release even young children who've been stung. Just a few years ago, those patients had intractable clonic seizures, hyperthermia, respiratory distress, and drowning secretions that required sedation, paralysis, intubation, and a helicopter flight to Tucson for a week's stay in the pediatric ICU.

The clinic property itself is single-story Spanish Colonial architecture originally built around an open square sun porch for the airing out of tuberculosis patients. It now has a shell of 1950s urbanity around it. The building and the property on which it sits are owned, as are all other things, by FMI. The equipment, including everything from X-ray machines and lab incubators to thermometers and baby blankets, are also owned, maintained, and replenished by the mine.

The staff are essentially contractors provided by a private consortium, Gila Health Resources, who work in partnership with FMI to care for the ill and care for the administrative tasks of billing and records and personnel.

As for the billing, similar to many modern healthcare enterprises, the clinic is often a money loser, especially the urgent care segment. FMI employees have healthcare coverage but any of the more transient contract workers in the supporting industries do not. When the clinic runs into the red, FMI makes up for the shortfall. That's a pragmatic move more than an altruistic one because any employer wants healthy, productive, present workers. Without the clinic, there'd be nothing. Thus, it's a worthwhile expenditure.

For all the weight the clinic bears, it is, in itself, a light and tight ship. There are eight physicians, five physician assistants, and a dedicated cadre of nurses and paramedics, all local. There's a small laboratory for basic bloodwork and an X-ray machine for trauma. There is no CT scanner or MRI machine, but there are mobile mammography, bone scan, and ultrasound providers who visit once or twice a month. Also visiting intermittently are a dentist, an ophthalmologist, and an optometrist. There is a doctor of pharmacy who staffs the clinic's pharmacy Monday through Friday. For patients who need other specialty care, a quick trip to Safford, about fifty minutes down the road, yields orthopedics, pediatrics, oncology, general surgery, and obstetrics.

There are four units of O-negative blood in the house and two ambulance crews staffed on a 24/7 basis. There are five ambulance rigs housed between the clinic and an outlying base. The mine fire department co-responds on motor vehicle accidents and other rescue situations. All of the fire department emergency response team staff are trained at least to the level of EMT-Basic. While their first priority is to be available for mining accidents, FMI supports off-premises response, as whoever requires rescue is undoubtedly a mine employee or one of their family members. Many of the nurses in the clinic cross-train and work on the ambulance. In a place like this, the more hats you're capable of wearing, the more valuable you are to your community in a tangible way.

Because of the paucity of resources, long ground transports to Safford or Tucson can rob the town of coverage for hours at a time. To that end, there's a well-lit helicopter pad just outside the clinic doors. Helicopter and fixed-wing emergency medical services are an integral part of the system, facilitating over one hundred fifty air transports per year. Folks here are so used to the bird landing that no one even glances at it anymore. Any major trauma, cardiac event, stroke or head injury, serious infection or sepsis, maternity emergency, or modestly critical pediatric patient gets a quick trip over the desert floor to waiting hospitals in Tucson or Phoenix.

Flying over Morenci, the temporal history of high production and low production can be traced by the style of homes, representing different decades of construction throughout the town. There are noticeable gaps and notable clusters. There's no city hall, because there's no incorporated city. And most of the land around this place is not privately owned. It's either state land, Bureau of Land Management, Native American reservation, or National Forest. Eight percent of Greenlee County is privately owned and about 7 of that 8 percent is owned by Freeport-McMoRan.

The mine built the school and the community center and the clinic and the fire station. The mine maintains the roads. And the mine owns every commercial enterprise in the community, save for one. The bar is owned by Michelle, who named it after herself and who pours me a cheap happy hour beer. At five-thirty on Friday evening, the joint is hopping. It's only a couple hundred yards from the exit road out of the mine and lies between the mine and all the houses. Prime real estate.

Most of the guys in here didn't even bother to take off their reflective safety vests. The percentage of men to women here is probably 66 percent to 33 percent by sight, an improvement from many industrial towns I've visited. That's probably thanks to the fact that the community, the mine, and one of two mining companies have been around for over one hundred years. Labor laws, combined with the growth of family units here, have diversified the gender distribution over time.

I only noticed one man camp, and it's identical to the camps I've seen in North Dakota, Alaska, and West Texas. In fact, it's run by the same company that is present in each of those oil field states. The camp is squeezed into one of the last remaining spots of undeveloped, mine-owned land, right between the slag heap and the railyard. The view out one window is ten lines of track holding crude oil tankers and dry bulk haulers and boxcars. Out the other window, a man-made plateau of processed rock holding a reservoir of tailing water.

The rest of Morenci is single-family homes and apartment buildings. Identical by decade. Rubber stamped. Each with a tiny, chain-link-fenced front yard, and each the same color.

The streets of Morenci are tiered, running a serpentine path along the sides of this wedding cake landscape. The town is built on some of the oldest mine tailings, and the placement of homes creates a hierarchy without hierarchy and a "can't get there from here" phenomenon of identical neighborhoods wrapping around artificial bluffs, with intervening ravines and washes that cannot be traversed except on foot. Even then, at some risk of snakebite or cactus entanglement.

These old tailings seem like natural earth now, except where they've eroded at the edges and at water runoff points. They are overshadowed and diminished by the monstrosity of the artificial mountain that is the working copper mine. As deep as the open pit goes, so high must the mountain be. All the earth moved to extract the copper must get redistributed. And it makes a mountain.

There is no horizon in Morenci. There are only tailings. There is no sunset here. There's only a glow behind the tailings. There is no landscape here, only tailings that look like land, just like land only different. Slightly more organized and slightly less chaotic than Mother Nature would have made it. To the people from here, it's just normal life. On the high school football field, there is only one goalpost. The teams only kick off in one direction, because, just beyond the end zone, there's only the hole. And no one's going all the way down there to fetch the football.

Can't Run & Never Will

A ghosted copper mine and Alaska's first X-ray machine
Kennecott, Alaska. Summer.

"Some places in the world should still be hard to get to," says the guide at Kennecott, Alaska. He makes his declaration in response to an angry tourist who is complaining about the condition of the road to get here.

Kennecott is definitely hard to get to. First, one must drive to Alaska, itself not an easy task. Then one takes the road to Valdez but stops short at Cordova. Next comes the "road" to Kennecott. It's not a road. It's seventy miles of stripped and abandoned railroad bed of the once gleaming Copper River & Northwestern Railway. While it was under construction, it was nicknamed the "Can't Run & Never Will" by skeptics who thought it would never be completed.

Alaska, along with parts of Canada, was one of many, many long road trips I took in and around the writing of this book. That old piece of train track, where the trees still form a train-shaped tunnel in some places, was one of the highlights of my time behind the wheel. It is not for the faint of heart nor the unprepared. But the reward, Kennecott and McCarthy, is worth the struggle.

Kennecott and the CR&NW Railway were built for one reason alone: copper. It was a company town perched at the toe of a glacier that is many stories smaller in height than it was in 1900. It was then that a patch of green "grass" up on the mountainside turned out to be the richest copper deposit in the world. In its heyday, Kennecott had everything: the world's first ammonia leaching plant, an indoor dairy, a self-contained power plant, and every creature comfort the company could muster. To attract and keep workers in an environment that was so isolated and cold that it could be madness-making, the Kennecott Copper Corporation built bachelor housing and a meat locker and a handful of small, single-family cottages.

There was a movie theater, a dance hall, a skating rink, a tennis court, a general store boasting the world's finest chocolate, and a hospital that contained the state's first X-ray machine. East coast doctors and nurses were brought in to keep the workers healthy. Steam from the power plant was run through pipes under the wooden sidewalks to keep them clear of ice and snow.

Now, though deserted, Kennecott is still a pleasant place to visit, if you're up for the trek. The old hospital still stands, notably the only whitewashed building in a cluster of otherwise barn-red structures (red paint, and its iron pigment, was the cheapest then, as it usually is now). The hospital has the same air of previous inhabitation and quiet drama that they all have. But now it's naked and exposed, open to the elements and tilting toward the stream, as if one day everything that happened there will get washed into the glacier to lie dormant.

As was typical of these remote mining camps, the hospital would have had one doctor and three nurses at any given time. It was built like a house, two stories plus a basement and an attic. It had beadboard-walled rooms that served as small wards. They had iron beds made up with hospital corners in the sheets. Half a century before the Americans with Disabilities Act, the hospital had a front porch and seven narrow steps leading up to the entrance. There was even a hospital dog, maybe one of the first therapy dogs in modern medicine. I suppose that the dog wasn't allowed in the small operating room with its rickety gurney and a machine to administer ether.

These days no one's allowed in it. It's leaning and creaking and totally creepy. Most of the glass is broken out and most of the whitewash is gone, leaving a smoky appearance that makes you wonder if there had been a fire. Every year, the spring flood of the small creek undermines more and more of the foundation, and soon it will fall.

After a tour through the old concentration mill, I sit to have a cold beverage and write my thoughts. It could be thirty years ago, or sixty, or even ninety. I sit at a table made of three hardwood planks nailed to four posts on a porch that overlooks the tiny main street of mud and gravel. There is dark beer in my glass, cold and refreshing after a day in the mill. A child rides by on a bicycle, ringing the bell on the handlebars. A young man beside me makes a call from a payphone, one of the few that remain in this country. An old Volkswagen van sits rusting next to a Model T. My cell phone rests beside me, anachronistic here.

In this town, in a bygone era, I would have had three options as a single woman. I could have been a schoolteacher, a secretary, or a nurse. The only other option was to get married. White-collar workers were allowed to come to Kennecott with their families. The bosses did a lot to keep them happy and brought in many of the creature comforts that the New Englanders and New Yorkers were accustomed to. Live music, tobacco, chocolate, steam-heated wooden sidewalks, and a screen on which they could play the latest movies were perks that went along with rank. The blue-collar workers who were the backbone of the mine had no such comfort. They lived in bunkhouses and worked long hours in an extraordinarily dangerous environment. The mill, where the copper slag arrived, ran twenty-four hours, three hundred sixty-three days a year, closing only for Christmas and the Fourth of July. Certain parts of the mill were heated by steam radiation to a balmy thirty-three degrees. Considering that temperatures outside could plummet to negative fifty, thirty-three was quite warm. The head boss is reputed to have said, "A cold worker is a hard worker because he's always trying to warm up."

Most miners only lasted six months. The longest tenures happened during the Depression, lasting thirteen months. A man's time was made arduous by the forbidding climate, the isolation, and the absence of his wife and children. For the ladies who arrived on the train as single women, they generally lasted one year before they were married. During that year, they were the most popular feature of each of the dances and socials. After that year, they retired from their service in industry and began their service in the home.

The children who were raised here during the mine's heyday were called Kennecott Kids. Now elderly themselves, they remember thinking the mountains framing the town were much smaller than they seem today. The mountains haven't changed that much, but the glacier has. It's gotten much smaller. The glacier once dwarfed the town, closing in the horizon and quickening the dusk. Now, the town sits about a hundred feet above it, with an expansive view of the valley that has been carved by the advancing and receding ice.

Kennecott, being a company town, was a dry town. McCarthy, walking distance down the train tracks, served as the source for liquor and women. Kennecott was primarily men with only a few living spaces for full families. For these, the company built small cottages in a row, only feet away from the railroad tracks. They could open the front door, take one step to cross the tiny porch, one step on dirt, and the next step up into the railcar.

In a memoir written by a child of that era, she recalls playing with her friends in one of the empty railcars as the train sat stranded by snow for several days, just outside the front door. They played with their dollies and their dishes and decided they wanted to play with Mommy's dishes as well. So, they took spoons and cups and plates from the kitchen and added them to their fantasy world inside the car. The next day, the snow had been cleared and the train was gone, along with their toys and, of course, Mommy's dishes. "Mother was not too happy about that," she said.

Dishes didn't always make the train, however. When the price of copper fell in 1938, the accountants in New York, running the numbers, realized one day that the mine and the mill and the town built to support it were no longer profitable. With the latest technology in place, as the owners always liked it, a phone call came into Kennecott with this message: "The last train leaves for Cordova in forty-eight hours. If you want out, you'd better be on it." Hundreds of men and dozens of families abandoned their lives, for some, the only lives they had known, in less than two days. When the first tourists wandered in years later, they found clothes in the closets, canned food in the cupboards, and dishes in the sinks. An entire town was ghosted virtually overnight.

Once the railroad was dismantled, there was no profitable way to salvage what was left in the mill and in the town. Copper buckets, copper spikes, hand tools, rail carts and heavy machinery, wooden vats, aluminum shaker tables, and even light bulbs still remain. A bucket of lard used to grease the machines hangs on its peg, covered in dust but still proudly blazing its emblem. I find old advertisements in the lodge that still boast about the "latest," greatest necessity of a woman's toilette, antiperspirant. I stand on the stoop of one of the cottages and hold a broom in my hand, which must have been laid aside when the news came in that the town, and life there, was ending. I swear it's still warm from the last hand to hold it.

Everywhere is the detritus of industry. Down over the bank, where the glacier now sits, I stumble upon hundreds and hundreds and hundreds of fifty-five-gallon barrels all rusted and weather-beaten and empty. They were tossed here and then forgotten. Just like the sock I find tossed into a corner of the machine shop, laden with dust now. This place is frozen in time in a frozen place in the world. And there is some unfinished business here.

A spirit lingers, and all who walk here feel it. It's the same spirit of once-was that is present in any of a thousand ghost towns across North America. Towns that were once lively, vibrant, and humming with opportunity. Now they're silent, with only the rusting of metal, the creaking of hinges, and the flaking of paint to mark the time.

We come, we take, we go, we repeat. And the places we've been are forever marked. Kennecott is marked by the tunnel through the trees, just exactly the size of the freight cars. Marked by the rare copper spike, left over from the tracks, that works its way northward through the graded roadbed to bite my tires. Marked by the old railroad trestle, tilted and rotting and adorned with ferns. Marked by the light bulbs still in their sockets and the bear hide drying in a barn. Marked by the two grizzly bears suddenly walking on the trail behind me and reminding me who actually rules this place.

And those doctors and nurses who cared for the townspeople, who left their own families behind so they could do some noble work, they're gone too. Only the old, whitewashed hospital remains. Waiting to collapse under the weight of time and snow, just like Kennecott.

The road to Kennecott isn't the first of Alaska's remote byways I've been on. I learned about that old ghost town and its abandoned hospital from the people at another hospital: the Alaska Native Medical Center (ANMC) in Anchorage. I completed a portion of my medical training in Alaska's system and was fortunate to have the opportunity to explore part of the state while I was there. To get to ANMC, I left Portland, Maine, in a two-door Ford Focus with a five-speed transmission, manual windows, no AC, and no radio. Fifteen days later I crossed from Canada's Yukon Territory into Alaska and thus accomplished a long-standing goal of visiting every state in the Union and every province of Canada.

I needed a new goal. So I decided to find the end of every road in Alaska. The road system only serves about 15 percent of the state, but, given that Alaska is almost two and a half times the size of Texas, it still covers a mind-bogglingly huge piece of geography. It's remarkably different north to south and east to west. And it changed me. Once you go to Alaska, you never really come all the way home.

There is something elemental about being reminded of your rightful place on the food chain. You feel your rung on that ladder in Alaska like nowhere else. Had man never harnessed water, never mastered fire, never learned to build shelter and preserve food, never fashioned weapons, we would not feel so smug today. Face-to-face, eye-to-piercing-eye with a bear, I understood, and was properly humbled.

Gazing upward at the soaring eagle, with his vision superior to mine by far, I felt earthbound and small. Standing in moose tracks the size of dinner plates, I knew I had not the speed to run for my life, nor the claws to defend it. My human skin is nothing without its manufactured coat of North Face. My agility and balance pale next to that of the Dall sheep, a thousand feet above me on an impossible cliff. The ease with which the Arctic wolf and the grizzly blend into their background, hard to spot even with high-powered optics, makes me feel clumsy and obvious.

I think of the night I lay in my tent on my way to Alaska, alone and human, in Northern Ontario. I awoke in the light of the arctic midnight and heard, felt, saw, and smelled a black bear, hundreds of pounds heavier and much hungrier than me, investigating my tent with her nose. It struck a fear so deep in me that no experience, no training, and no level of preparedness could stifle the whimper that stole from my lips. Nothing at that moment could have quieted the heart beating in my ears so hard I felt it would burst from my chest, so fast that my vision blurred with it. Each snort from her nose felt like hot breath on my neck. Each footstep in the gloomy midnight felt as if it was on my very skin. Terror is not an adequate word for what I felt. I could smell my own fear in the sweat that threatened to drown me in my sleeping bag. Do I lie still? Do I shout and blow my whistle? Do I clutch my knife and my shovel in my hands and prepare to fight, if necessary, to the death? I've been so careful, so diligent and disciplined.

I've not worn perfume for weeks. Everything that touches my body is unscented, even my laundry detergent. Not an ounce of food has touched this tent, ever. I washed my hands and my face and changed clothes after dinner. There is no toothpaste, no bug spray, no chapstick, no face cream within fifty yards of me. My food is stored in waterproof bags, inside a cooler in a locked a car, a thousand feet away from me. But it's happening. She's outside, she has young, and she's hungry. And I'm here all alone. There are no other tenters, no other campers so early in the season. The caretakers are asleep, tucked into their log cabin separated from me by woods and distance and precious time. So, what is left but to lie still, struggling to control my breath, stifle my shudders, and reign in the soft, whispered grunts of fear that seem to come from someone else but are, in fact, made in me? I sound like prey. And that is what I am here. Undeniably.

It is that fear, that feeling of being prey, that moves humans to come together in communities. We come together to make shelter, to make food, and to entertain ourselves. For as long as there have been villages there has also been sport.

In Alaska, on the Fourth of July every year, a marathon takes place. It's not a traditional marathon, which is fitting, as this is not a traditional place. Seward, Alaska, on the blue waters of Prince William Sound, doesn't freeze in during the winter. It is an ideal port that was going to be the "big city" of Alaska before Anchorage outgrew it. The marathon started just after the turn of the century and has earned its place as the third-oldest footrace in America. But it is by far the most unique.

Rather than 26 miles, this event measures a paltry 3.1. But what it lacks in length, it makes up for in altitude. The race goes 3,022 feet up a 70 percent grade. This is the Seward Mount Marathon. Three heats of competitors run from downtown, up the hill, past the hospital to a trail fit for athletic mountain goats, not for humans. In the morning, the children run. Boys and girls together, ranging in age from seventeen to what appears to be seven. Some of them are so young that I feel like I should call Child Protective Services. They are battered, bloody, and exhausted, stumbling their way back down the street. But these are Alaska's children. And they are all smiles. Later, they'll be walking around downtown eating reindeer dogs and slurping ice cream, with their shorts still muddy and torn.

After the kids run to the halfway mark and back, the adults get their turn. First the women, then the men. This race is difficult to enter. You either earn your slot or get drawn in a lottery the night before. These folks are professionals. The ones who finish early are lean and light. As sure-footed as a tank and as spry as a cat. The overly-muscled and the under-conditioned come across the finish line many minutes behind the low-fat, skim-milk racers at the head of the pack. The hard part, going up, slows them down to a vertical walk. That's followed by a four-pointed scramble up the last thousand vertical feet. Hard dirt, sharp gravel, sheer cliffs, and severe switchbacks do all they can to slow the pace. But the truly terrifying part, for me as a spectator at least, is the way down. The ascent takes nearly fifty minutes, the descent a mere ten. The runners cross a ridge over to the northeastern face and spend the first eight hundred feet or so literally sliding on their shorts down what is left of the patchy, icy, brown snow. Like a frozen Slip 'N Slide, the chute flings them out onto the impossibly steep, rocky downhill that is, at this point, still above tree line. Not even a low-lying bush can pad a fall or abort a tumble.

Once they're into the tree line, the runners basically free fall the remainder of the route. Their feet just barely break their speed and prevent their demise.

There is an ambulance set up at the point where the trail meets the road. There are fully-loaded stretchers two hundred feet up, at the halfway point and at the summit. The emergency room is on the route and the medical helicopter waits at the bottom. The crew, in their flight suits, watch the runners come by. I watch them bring one injured racer down.

As the athletes lose altitude, they gain bruises, road rash, chipped teeth, blisters, pulled muscles, sprained ankles, broken bones, head injuries, and heart attacks. It makes me glad I'm not working.

As the two leaders cross the finish line, almost neck and neck with each other and a few minutes under an hour of an all-out sprint, they both go to ground. They hug the pavement as if it's the softest mattress they've ever laid upon. They pant, but otherwise they are still. Drained. Their faces start out contorted with pain, then smooth out until they portray the purest of exhaustion. After a few minutes, when they've caught their breath a bit, a look of utter peace and rapture washes across their features. As the winner is dragged to her feet by her husband, she clutches him, her head resting on his shoulder, her feet barely skimming the ground as he supports her weight. Her children and the photographers gather around her and she lets out a cheer. "Woo! . . . Woo-hoo," she shouts. Tears pour down her husband's face and the faces of several onlookers. At that moment, it makes sense to me. I get it. This is why they run. The elation of conquering a giant. David laughing in the face of Goliath. Perhaps it's not so crazy after all.

At the other end of the state, up on the Arctic Ocean, people also come together, but for work, not for entertainment. Of all the roads I've driven, the one I'm most proud of is the Dalton Highway up to Prudhoe Bay. Driving it, there were moments I felt I might drive off the end of the earth. I was so alone that I felt like the last pickle in the barrel. Then, as the fog rolled across the tundra, as I worked my way down the North Slope, I became so disoriented I could scarcely tell if I was climbing or descending. The sun broke through and presented me with the clearest blue skies and piercing sunshine that I'd seen in months.

Once the horizon reappeared, the tundra flattened out and opened up. It was the two weeks of autumn when the mosquitoes were gone, and the snow had yet to arrive. So much changes from minute to minute in that place. On my way home, southbound only one day after heading up, the tundra exploded with color. It was even more brilliant than the day before. As striking as any New England autumn, the colors don't tower overhead. Instead, they spread out on the ground as far as you can see.

Anyone who has sat around a campfire and been mesmerized by the flames knows these colors. It's as if someone lit the prairie on fire, but instead of leaving a charred blackness behind, the flames laid down the shades they had burned. Red. Cranberry red, fire-engine red, deep mahogany, and carnation pink. Orange. Pumpkin orange, burnt orange, and tangerine. Yellow. Champagne yellow, banana yellow, and lemon meringue. Green. Emerald, sea foam, and forest. Purple. Lilac and lavender and the hot plum of fireweed.

These rolling hills are painted with jewel tones and when the sun shines behind them, everything sparkles like it's been glazed with honey. I can hardly take my eyes off it because I'm afraid the next time I look it will be gone.

The season is so brief that it nearly breaks my heart to look at it. It makes me want to run across these open plains and clutch the earth to my chest in giant armfuls, breathing it, tasting it, hearing the great, deafening silence of it.

There is only one road, so it's impossible to get lost. The only people on the road are professional, well-trained, and experienced drivers. There is no alcohol allowed and all "slope" workers get drug tested frequently. So everyone on the road is sober. They all know that being unsafe or careless will cost them their jobs, or perhaps their lives. Everyone helps those in trouble because they know they could be the next one who needs a helping hand. A CB radio is virtually required for travel here, and drivers coordinate their own traffic for the length of the road.

"Southbound, Ice Cut," a driver calls out as we crest the hill approaching a valley where the Sag River cuts a swath known as the Ice Cut.

"Northbound four-wheeler, Happy Valley," I announce as I approach another blind turn.

"Heads up, caribou crossing, sir."

"Thank you, ma'am, safe trip."

For the rare hunter or tourist like myself, space on this road is gifted, not righted. It must be negotiated, not demanded. This road exists for one purpose: to move equipment and supplies to and from the North Slope oil field and the Trans-Alaska Pipeline. That's it. That's why they call it the haul road. As for the drivers, if you slow them down, you cost them money. If you get in their way or lose control, you may damage property. You may waste money and resources. You may destroy valuable habitat in a fragile environment. Or you may take a life, including your own. Just like the road to Kennecott, this road is not for everyone. It shouldn't be. But for those who do it carefully, with adequate planning and a respectful attitude, it proves to be a challenge worth taking. The road was built for oil. There's a clinic in Prudhoe Bay that was also built by the oil companies. But I didn't come here for it. I came here for the road.

"So, now where do you go?"

His voice, the voice of a trucker I met in the chow hall, crackles over the CB radio, sounding distant in space and time, though it is neither.

"What's next?"

We leave Prudhoe Bay, southbound, at the same time and we follow each other, alone together for miles. We are connected by a short wave antenna and the coincidence of reaching for the last piece of pie in the cafeteria at the same time.

I didn't set out on the road to find healing or peace. But somewhere in the miles, they found me. Perhaps it is the hours I spent with only my own voice for company. Perhaps it is the universality and individuality of life I found between San Diego and Newfoundland. Perhaps it is the human spirit I found between Key West and Prudhoe Bay. Perhaps it is the rhythm and texture of the road as it rolls beneath me, anchoring and yet freeing me. Maybe it was learning to overcome fear. Or maybe it was just time.

It takes time to drive through all fifty states. It takes time to travel every province in Canada. It takes time to find the end of every road in Alaska. Just as a heart takes time to heal, a spirit takes time to mend. At some milepost, I learned to look only forward and not count those behind. At some river bridge, I learned the only way to cross it was to cross it. At some state line, I learned that the boundaries we set are artificial and can be redrawn. At some rest stop, I learned the value of coffee and conversation and human connection. At some toll booth, I learned there is no cost as great as wasted time. And at some coastline, I was rinsed clean. Where to now? Anywhere. I fear no road.

Under Pressure

Profile of an oil town that's done it right
Artesia, New Mexico. Spring.

At over seventy-three thousand square feet and twenty million dollars, the Artesia Public Safety Complex in Artesia, New Mexico, is impressive as a structure. The relatively new station brings the fire department, police department, sheriff's office, state police, and probation and municipal court all under one expansive and well-designed roof. With the vision of two public safety chiefs, J.D. Hummingbird of Artesia Fire Department and Don Raley of Artesia Police Department, as well as the help of Municipal Judge Kaye Kiper (retired) and the support of Mayor Phillip Burch, the new house stands as a metaphor for the cooperation, innovation, and forward thinking the city's leaders embody.

The complex serves as a source of pride for a community that is blossoming at a healthy pace in the midst of the largest oil boom since Illinois Well #3 hit black gold here in 1924. An artesian well does not require a pumping apparatus. Instead, a pipe is inserted vertically into a pool of fluid (oil or water) that is lying at an angle to gravity. Like a river flowing downhill, but in the substrata. The downward hydrostatic pressure of the fluid "uphill" of the pipe's orifice forces the oil up to ground level, up the pipe.

In the twenty-first century, hydraulic fracturing (fracking) and directional drilling have revolutionized the oil and gas industry, changing the landscape forever. People tend to have strong opinions on the process, especially if they don't fully understand it. But there is no disputing that unprecedented amounts of revenue come out of it because it's more efficient. A community can choose to fight that or choose to derive benefit from it.

Artesia, New Mexico, is an example of how to create a well-funded, safe, sustainable community in the midst of a population explosion that could potentially be chaotic and destructive. Mayor Burch smiles and tells me, "Artesia is special because the citizens expect it to be special."

And there's the crux of the issue. A sense of ownership and community pride motivates the town's residents to care about infrastructure. Which in turn, promotes philanthropy. Both the mayor and the chief of police said that most things happen in Artesia simply because people, real people, talk. They just ask. "It's not something you do. It's something that happens," says Burch.

Business leaders, city government, and public safety officials see each other around town, on the golf course, at church, and, most importantly, at high school football games. Football is a big deal here, as the water tower at the edge of town, emblazoned with state championship years, can attest. As can the relatively new fire chief. Shortly after arriving in town, Chief Hummingbird joked about building the new Public Safety Complex in the middle of the "Bulldog Bowl." He was quickly brought up to speed on the importance of football to Artesians, and he went on to become New Mexico's Fire Chief of the Year while dreaming up a new station that would grace the cover of *Fire Chief* magazine.

As I talk to people throughout the town, from the firefighters —lieutenants and captains to the administrative assistants—to the mayor, the chamber of commerce, and the chief of police, they speak of Chief Hummingbird with reverence and pride. He changed an entire culture, shifted a paradigm, and created a well-trained, well-equipped, unified, and professional department on which the town can depend. He's directed a 1,000 percent increase in the annual budget, written good grants, been a regular presence in the governor's office, and encouraged a "pretty awesome" relationship with the city council. By planning fifteen years ahead, he helped to set the tone for infrastructure development in the region.

The laurels don't rest solely on Hummingbird's shoulders, however. He's quick to point out that Chief Raley has also shaken things up, to the detriment of local gangs and potential drug dealers who were looking to reap the benefit of a boomtown economy.

Drug crime and property crime rates have gone down, even though the population has come up. Chief Raley attributes this to several community-based efforts. The Artesia Police Department has a significant presence in the local schools and has become a national model for school resource officers. The students graduating this year have known local law enforcement through the school, in a nonpunitive way, since they were in kindergarten, and that has made a tangible dent in gang activity.

This small town department, headed by a chief who spent most of his career as a detective, has state-of-the-art DNA identification technology and an evidence bunker that officers from all over the country come to marvel at and envy. The department has prosecuted and convicted more than a dozen cases of auto burglary (burglary, not even auto theft) using DNA technology.

Artesia Police Department officers often go door to door, bringing community policing directly to the people they serve. The department identifies a problem in a specific neighborhood thanks to diligent and modern record keeping, and they make house calls, unsolicited, to every home in the affected area. These officers get woven into the fabric of the community and from that "there comes to be a certain certainty that you're going to get caught," says Chief Raley.

His officers have some pretty sophisticated tools for catching folks. The field investigators are equipped with digital cameras that, even though they take pretty good pictures, look downright blurry next to the images produced by the new FARO panoramic digital crime scene scanner. The FARO can be set up in the middle of a crime scene and snap a series of images that enable super-precise measurements, CAD reproduction, and three-dimensional rendering for presentation in court. It cuts the time needed to process a crime scene by more than half, which gets officers back into the community more quickly. It's unusual for a department of this size to have one, but they raised the right funds to get it.

There are only so many officers and their time is in high demand. But it's better than it used to be. Now, thirty-four out of thirty-five available sworn positions are filled, compared with only nineteen filled spots when Raley became chief in 2006. Many communities, in similar situations to Artesia's, have had difficulty recruiting certified, qualified, experienced officers. "The key," says Chief Raley, "is that we started to turn people away. By saying no we got more yesses."

By that he means that his department has gotten away from the "warm body" mentality of simply filling positions to have names on the roster. Good officers want to work with other good officers, even if it means they are fewer in number, rather than serving fewer shifts alongside people who can't be trusted.

Another component of Artesia's feeling of relative calm and safety is the advent of FLETC, the Federal Law Enforcement Training Center, which was established here just after September 11, 2001. It's a multiagency, live-in training academy for the US Border Patrol, US Air Marshals, and Bureau of Indian Affairs Police. Raley jokes, "Artesia is probably the only city in America where you can see a group of ten young men standing on a street corner at ten o'clock at night and feel completely safe." He laughs, "Because they're all law enforcement."

The partnership with these federal agencies also includes the Regional Emergency Dispatch Authority (REDA) housed on the FLETC campus, a driver training facility on site, and a city-wide emergency alerting system that includes siren and broadcast towers around town, activated at REDA, and able to warn citizens of impending danger such as a tornado, flood, fire, hazardous materials situation, or terrorist threat. Verbal messages can provide specific instructions to the locals, expediting the communications process.

Despite all the bells and whistles, the best policing still happens at a community, street level. The department holds regular "Briefings in the Park" and an annual Child Safety Fair where the kids can go through a mini police academy. If they "graduate," they are entered to win one of thirty to forty bicycles donated by local businesses. They also celebrate a National Night Out during which the entire town eats for free. It gives local law enforcement officers a chance to be present in a low-stress, positive, approachable way. All this comes about and gets funded through simple face-to-face conversation on a human level. "We just ask," says Chief Raley.

His hope for the future is that his agency can keep pace with the forecasted population growth, and that as more hotels and short-term apartments are built, that the resultant, somewhat transient population doesn't detract from those invested in the community. And like any law enforcement leader, Raley is concerned about drug use, especially stimulants such as cocaine and methamphetamine, occasionally found in blue-collar communities where people are trying to stay awake for work.

By training together, and by mounting joint SWAT and negotiations teams with the Eddy County Sheriff's Office and the New Mexico State Police, the Artesia Police Department is ready to act when the need arises. And appropriately equipped to do so, thanks to the emphasis the city's leaders have placed on public safety. After all, most folks in Artesia are just "a hardworking group of people who believe that what they do provides for their families and their community," as they are characterized by Mayor Burch.

Burch grew up in Artesia. Then, as many young people do, he left the area for thirty-five years. That's typical of the "brain drain" common to this part of the country. However, Burch feels that tide turning. Folks are starting to feel good about remaining in Artesia because there is a strong sense of community and of family values. Those values help keep the major export (young people) to a minimum. Burch feels very fortunate to be occupying the mayor's desk at this time in history. "There are so many positives [in Artesia] that I'd have to really screw up to hurt that," he smiles.

There is a strong sense of regionalism now in southeast New Mexico that fuels good partnerships and the sharing of innovation between community leaders of neighboring towns, especially between Artesia and Roswell, New Mexico. Ten city representatives from Artesia and ten from Roswell travel to Washington, DC, every year together, and a lot of forward-thinking planning happens on those plane rides.

The mayor finds it helpful to know that the same concerns he has for his town are shared by others. He breaks these concerns down into two categories: those over which there is some local control and those over which there is none. Of the things he's able to influence, his biggest worry is the education of Artesia's children. "The Artesia public school system is one of the better ones in the state, but the state's overall education system is poor." As for things beyond the span of local control, "there are a lot of state and federal agencies that pass regulation, which no one votes on, that impact the oil and gas business." And often, those regulations are put forth by people who've never visited the region or engaged in a dialogue about their concerns at a local level.

The same applies to the aviation and nuclear industries that support the economy of neighboring towns in the region. So the mayor and city council do what they can to diversify and stabilize their own economy. And that's crucial for a one-industry town, diversification. One way they've done that in Artesia is with healthcare. Artesia General Hospital has made dramatic strides and is poised to become a regional center providing specialty care closer to home and within the borders of New Mexico.

Historically, if a patient has needed specialty care, from orthopedics to cardiac or pulmonary care, or even some simple procedures, they've had to travel to Lubbock, Texas, 170 miles away. That adds extra expense and worry to the patient and their family and often ties up a valuable ambulance for hours at a time. Being able to offer these services in Artesia is not only better for the patient but also provides quality, steady jobs for both skilled and unskilled workers.

Artesia has already made strides in advancing healthcare on the front lines, thanks to a casual conversation that happened on the golf course between Fire Chief Hummingbird and Marla Hardy, RN, base manager for the medical helicopter that now lives at the public safety complex. While the southeast region of New Mexico has been covered by helicopter and fixed-wing bases in Roswell and Hobbs, there had never previously been a helicopter based out of Artesia. And given that less than three months into the program the flight crews are already averaging one flight per day (a lot for a new program), the location is probably even more important than anyone could have predicted. It's already the fourth-busiest aircraft in Tri-State's fleet and may soon catapult to number one as regional hospitals and first responders get more familiar with the bird.

It's an Agusta A119 Koala staffed with a flight paramedic and a flight nurse and flown by seasoned pilots, almost all of whom have decades of military experience. The helicopter sits just outside the fire department's apparatus bay and the crews share living spaces with the firefighters.

Artesia Fire Department provides emergency medical services to the town as the primary transporting ambulance and each firefighter is trained at least to the EMT-Basic level, the majority to the EMT-Paramedic level. Quartering together with the air medical crews helps each agency better understand the capabilities and needs of the other. Therefore, calls are run more efficiently and safely. Also, since both agencies regularly interact with the hospital, there are lots of opportunities for training and learning.

In all, the under-one-roof interaction between firefighters, air medical staff, and city and county law enforcement makes for a unified team of public safety professionals who embody the spirit of cooperation and community for which Artesia is becoming known. It's a model that other blossoming boomtowns could emulate. Mayor Burch acknowledges that Artesia will likely outpace its larger neighbors in growth over the next twenty years. He hopes that it will look much like it does today, just bigger. He hopes that city government and local business will retain the cooperative efforts that have helped to plump up local infrastructure, advance the arts and education, and support philanthropic reinvestment here. In a reflection of their name, Artesians are rising under pressure.

The WIPP Site

Caring for those who care for our radioactive waste
Carlsbad, New Mexico. Late spring.

There was a one-in-ten-thousand chance of a leak. Maybe even one in a million. Those were the numbers calculated after twenty-five years of research into the spill-proof, leakproof, puncture-proof, fire-resistant, and crush-resistant storage containers for radioactive waste that travel across the country to the Waste Isolation Pilot Plant (WIPP) in southeast New Mexico. The WIPP site, twenty-six miles southeast of Carlsbad, is a geological repository for nuclear waste—mostly contaminated equipment as opposed to high-level reactor cores—that is the industrial byproduct of weapons research and development in the United States. It's a salt deposit 2,150 feet below ground, with zero sources of drinking water nearby and essentially no inhabitants until the Carlsbad city limits.

There were over two decades of research into construction, safety, environmental impact, shipping routes, system redundancy, and disaster mitigation before the first shipment of waste ever hit the front doors in 1999. Now, there are fifty-six rooms carved into the salt deposit, each a hundred yards in length, storing over 74,000 cubic meters of sealed material. That's over ten thousand shipments.

The WIPP site was designed for about forty or fifty years of accepting shipments to reach full capacity, after which the rooms will be encased in thirteen layers of soil and concrete. After that, Mother Nature will do the rest of the isolation work through something referred to as "salt creep." The salt formation is slowly, constantly moving like shifting sand dunes, only at a much slower pace, responding to changes in pressure from geothermal forces. And in about seventy-five years, the salt in the walls, floors, and ceilings of the mine will essentially close in, locking the waste in place, impermeably, forever. Or at least for the ten thousand years of predictable decay of the radioactive waste there, most of which is plutonium and americium.

In the fifteen years that have passed since the first load arrived, the safety record at WIPP has been impeccable. But it's that one-in-ten-thousand incident, along with standard-fare hazards, trauma, and fire potential for which the emergency services technicians (ESTs) of the on-site fire brigade prepare. And it's Patrick Kirksey's job as the emergency preparedness coordinator at WIPP to make sure his team is prepared to respond to a wide variety of service requests that, on the surface, are as straightforward as any industrial jobsite, but that get exponentially more difficult once you're in "the hole."

Greater than 95 percent of the three or four calls that the sixteen ESTs run each month are medical in nature. The WIPP site employs about one thousand people under the Department of Energy, but only about three hundred of those are on-site at peak operations. A minority of the three hundred are actually working underground and only during daytime hours. Most of those folks are young, healthy, and screened with annual physical exams. So their preexisting medical conditions such as high blood pressure, diabetes, or seizure disorders are well known ahead of time.

When an employee does need assistance, the ESTs are trained, licensed, and equipped to provide EMT-Intermediate level care, though several of the staff are trained to the paramedic level through prior employers. They have one pumper, one heavy rescue truck, and one surface ambulance in their fleet. It's bare bones, but adequate. There is also an underground, all-terrain-type "ambulance" that can fit in one of three elevator cages that connect the mine to the surface on a five-minute trip. The smallest of the elevators is considered an escape shaft "for use only in extreme emergency," and is just large enough that a patient who is well strapped to a backboard or stokes basket can be propped up at a 45° angle and evacuated to the surface. It's a scenario the ESTs regularly rehearse, just in case.

Working below grade presents additional challenges beyond the space and time constraints of the elevators. Every surface is made of salt. Radios don't work and ventilation is paramount. There are teams of engineers monitoring the structural integrity of the rooms, the air quality, and the radiation levels, which are essentially lower than radiation levels found above ground in the normal atmosphere.

Communication is handled "over the wire" through a system of hardwired, party-line mine phones placed throughout the underground and surface-level buildings. The central monitoring room, with half a dozen communications specialists on duty, handles all staff communications at the site. This includes mine phones, surface radios used by ESTs and security officers above ground, surrounding city dispatch center interaction, and environmental monitoring systems. They also track, via real-time GPS, any truck from around the country that is bringing waste to the WIPP site.

The central monitoring staff, along with the ESTs, are responsible for about twenty-five structures on the 1-square-mile campus, which is situated on 16 square miles of secured desert scrub. The facility also has mutual aid agreements with Carlsbad, Hobbs, and Jal Fire Departments, all in southeastern New Mexico, for co-response to motor vehicle accidents on several of the surrounding highways. It's up to the discretion of the shift manager on duty whether to respond to those cross-coverage requests. Their primary obligation is to protect the industrial complex. However, because of the remote nature of the surrounding landscape, long response times from nearby cities, and the high-speed intensity of some of the collisions, their added response effort may truly make a difference in patient survival.

All ESTs are certified firefighters in addition to EMTs, and all security personnel are cross-trained in fire suppression. The full-time staff can be quickly augmented by a group of volunteer firefighters whose full-time job description is something else entirely, but who may be on-site when an incident occurs. They have trained alongside their EST counterparts.

Because the WIPP site is such an isolated, monitored, and highly-controlled facility, fires and hazardous materials incidents are exceedingly rare. As are incidents of physical threat, since all employees and visitors are closely screened upon entry and exit of the facility. That said, there is electrical equipment, motorized machinery, fuel, and heavy equipment, all of which carries the same risk as it would in your local shopping plaza. More commonly, routine health issues arise such as headaches, intestinal distress, upper respiratory infections, allergic reactions, and minor trauma. Most of these are addressed in the clinic. The clinic is staffed Monday through Friday, eight hours per day, by two experienced registered nurses. There are no physicians, physician assistants, or nurse practitioners on-site. There are two small exam rooms in the clinic with available 12-lead electrocardiography and stocked with advanced cardiac life support medications, an Automated External Defibrillator, and minor pain-relief medications.

For a higher level of care, patients can be transported by the WIPP ambulance to Carlsbad Medical Center, twenty-six miles away. If paramedic-level care is required, the ESTs from WIPP can request an advanced life support intercept from Carlsbad Fire Department. That means that one of the ambulances from

Carlsbad will meet them on the highway and send a paramedic over to the WIPP rig. For the rare critical patient at WIPP, a medical helicopter from Artesia or Hobbs can arrive within minutes.

Any time workers are in the underground repository, there is at least one EST underground along with the all-terrain ambulance. They are part of an entire team dedicated to safety. They facilitate prework and post-work safety briefings, constant monitoring, and a litany of safety procedures. Anyone, anywhere on the facility, is empowered to initiate a work stoppage in the event they see, hear, or feel something unsafe. And there are clear isolation, segregation, and evacuation plans in place, including sequestering or rerouting ventilation components, sealing off rooms, and evacuating the repository.

A fire and then a radiation leak occurred on Valentine's Day, 2014, and essentially shut down the facility for the foreseeable future. At the writing of this chapter, no humans have yet been allowed below grade, and remote probes are being lowered into the mines to take video recordings, temperature and radiation readings, and air samples. In the next few days, the first engineers may descend to try and figure out the cause of this sentinel event. Already it has perpetuated standing misconceptions held by the public about high levels of radiation exposure and high cancer rates. The leak has prompted an appropriate halt to the admittance of outside visitors, just prior to my planned visit. What are the chances? One in ten thousand.

As I've done elsewhere along the path of research, when my well-laid plans are interrupted like this, I get back behind the wheel and drive on. I'm headed east and south, toward Houston, where I'm not going to spend much time. I don't enjoy the place. It feels quite plastic and manufactured to me. But I have to drive through it to get to Clear Lake, Texas, which is where the NASA installation lives. My next interview will be with the physician who cares for the astronauts.

Something that surprised me about Houston is that there is a system of underground walking tunnels, like a subway without the trains. It connects most of the buildings of downtown. And it's bizarre to me. It's a way to walk from office to office without having to endure the searing heat and humidity of summer. It's similar to Montreal's tunnel system, a footprint almost as large as that above ground, which allows people to dodge the depths of winter.

There are clothing stores and restaurants and barber shops and dentists. There are law offices and banks and cell phone stores. There's a footrace rush hour at the end of the day, looking nearly as busy as any NYC Financial District street at five o'clock. It's weird. It's unexpected and mildly claustrophobic. What I don't understand, though, is what happens down there during the hurricanes and the resulting floods that seem to strike Houston at least once per decade, foreseeably more often as our climate destabilizes.

In 2008, an old classmate of mine lost both her parents to Hurricane Ike when, as they belatedly tried to evacuate their high-rise apartment building, they made the fatal mistake of taking the elevator instead of the stairs. Someone else had also made the mistake of failing to disable the elevators with the fire department key. They descended to the parking garage, in the basement of the building, and the doors opened to a completely flooded space, the water rushing inside and entombing them like a submarine compartment with an open bulkhead. Though it appears they tried to push the button for the first floor, the elevator machinery couldn't lift the weight of a car full of water, and there they died.

I can envision each of these tunnels as a postapocalyptic scuba diving habitat, where divers with fins and flashlights can browse the flooded bookstore and pretend to dine at flooded food court tables. But then again, there's something wrong with my brain. I'm a product of this work that I do and work that I've done in the past. I see the potential for disaster everywhere. I can't turn it off. And I see it in gruesome detail, little vignettes playing out in my head at the slightest provocation.

A woman holding a child by the hand and pushing a stroller wanders a little close to the edge of the subway platform and I gasp, seeing how close the toddler is to falling down onto the tracks. When they escape that potential disaster and ramble on down the platform, I'm still there, planning my response. I'd pull the stroller away from the edge and recruit the man standing next to me to jump down to the tracks and hand me the kid. I'd tell the woman beside me to run to the end of the platform and try to signal the train to stop if it approaches. And I worry about how we'd get the man back up on the platform, knowing there's no place to put your feet and boost yourself up, anticipating a train bursting around the corner at just that moment. Who the fuck thinks like that?

I'm out at a bar and people are dancing. It's a small space and there are candles on the tables. There's a tall girl in a dress, dancing. She's drunk. She loses control and careens toward the table. I gasp. As she dances away unscathed, in my mind, I see her falling backwards over the obstacle, landing on her back and breaking her neck on the wooden bench. I see the candle catching her long linen skirt on fire and racing up the curtains next to the window, a Coconut Grove scene for the modern age of fire prevention.

I see water on the bathroom floor and I picture all the old people I've found broken and screaming, or broken and dead, throughout the years. I've never fallen in the bathroom, but I must've responded to at least 150 people who have in my years in the field. I've never cut my finger off in the kitchen slicing a bagel or in my woodshop working with the lathe, but I've picked up at least half a dozen fingertips and put them on ice.

I've never had second degree burns from a firecracker or a camping stove or a barbeque grill, but I've treated at least twenty people who did and that's why I won't light any of them. I've never broken my leg on a hiking trail, but I've rescued five people who did, and that's why it takes me so long to hike down a mountain.

I can't stop those visions from popping up in my head and at times it's crippling. For years, I thought I was the only one. Now, I know that I'm not. For years, I got angry with the people in my life who couldn't understand my behavior. Now, I know that they never will. Now, I use self-distraction techniques to change the picture in my head. And as the moment passes, I say to those around me who can't understand why I'm so uptight, "Sorry . . . PTSD."

And that's enough. I'm not alone.

What Happens if an Astronaut Ejaculates?

Aerospace medicine and the world's astronauts
Johnson Space Center, Clear Lake, Texas. Late Spring.

"So . . . what happens, then, if an astronaut ejaculates on the International Space Station?"

I never pictured myself standing at Mission Control in NASA's Johnson Space Center (JSC) asking the medical director that question. But here I am and there it is, out of my mouth and traversing the space between us too quickly for me to reel it back in. By this point in our day, Dr. William Tarver and I have already covered a significant amount of territory regarding fluids in the absence of gravity, no insignificant variable. The long and short of his answer is, "I don't know, and I don't want to know."

But Dr. Tarver knows most everything else about the six astronauts currently on low-earth orbit aboard the International Space Station (ISS). The National Aeronautics and Space Administration comes with its own specialized medical establishment, and the doctors who work here tend to do so for life. Some of them come from a military background like Dr. Tarver, a flight surgeon in the air force. Others come here as residents from the

University of Texas Medical Branch (UTMB) Aerospace Medicine Residency Program. They are often recruited by word of mouth from one person already in the system to another.

Once bitten by the space bug, there's no looking back. A job here, caring for the world's space travelers, comes with the excitement and wonder of taking part in the nation's most forward-thinking and exciting research. It comes with bragging rights and swagger and an utterly unique relationship with the men and women of childhood adoration and Hollywood fantasy.

Dr. Tarver is maybe the last person I'd expect to brag, and there's certainly no swagger to his relaxed southern stroll. He has an easy drawl and a patient speech pattern. He's one of those kind souls that immediately inspires confidence and takes the urgency out of even the most serious circumstances. He's measured. And probably the perfect counterpoint to the fighter-pilot type A personalities that often occupy jobs in aerospace.

Therein lies the change in the astronaut population over the last decade. Originally, the astronauts were all pilots, carefully selected for their fitness, their prowess, and their balls. The shuttle missions, like the missions that proceeded them, were of short duration, two weeks or less. They were wind sprints, and the shuttle astronauts were sprinters. Now, astronauts spend months at a time aboard the ISS, typically eight to twelve, with the longest American stint by Scott Kelly at 340 days. Russian cosmonaut Valery Polyakov spent 438 days aboard the Mir portion of the space station before it was joined to the American half. Peggy Whitson has spent the longest time aboard as a woman with 289 consecutive days in 2016–2017, but a total of 665 days on several missions.

These men and women are a much different demographic: explorers, scientists, marathoners. They're just as disciplined as their predecessors, but more studious. And still numbering only a few. There have only been about 560 people in space ever (two-thirds of those American), so, as a patient cohort, they are too small to reach any meaningful statistical significance for study. The only research point that's been proven is that astronauts are more likely to die in space-vehicle accidents than non-astronauts.

Despite their relatively small number, the health and welfare of each astronaut is extensively studied, measured, and trended. There are usually six scientists aboard the ISS at any given time. Three astronauts make the trip to and from the craft, so there are always three people up there. On my visit to JSC, there are three Russians, two Americans, and one Brit on board. That's a typical representation. Half the crew (three) will be American and two will be Russian, or vice versa. The other slot will be filled with someone from Canada, Japan, Great Britain, or the European Union. Their home, the International Space Station, took 136 missions to assemble. Just prior to my visit, they had been on a space walk to move the Pressurized Mating Adapter to the front, or the "head end," of the ISS.

There are more countries participating in space research than ever before, and there's the addition of more private, commercial interaction. Thus, the layout of the ISS is being modified to allow for more diverse docking capabilities.

Astronauts and cosmonauts alike get to and from the ISS in the Soviet-built Soyuz vehicle, essentially the taxicab for astronauts. It's a small, efficient, resilient, claustrophobia-inducing bullet perched on top of the Soyuz rocket, the most dependable in the world. And it still looks like 1961 in its electronics and even its upholstery. Standing next to a Soyuz in Building 9, I marvel at a handcrafted leather door bag that holds some sort of emergency equipment. The working unit is at the Cosmodrome in Kazakhstan.

My version of the Soyuz is propped up in the Space Vehicle Mockup Facility next to the excruciatingly accurate full-size replica of the ISS. All astronauts train here, and I see a few of them moving around inside it on my visit. On the "floor" of the ISS mockup, there are realistic, high-definition photographs of the equipment that would get stomped upon here on Earth, but that would just be another working surface in the weightlessness of space, where there is no floor.

This practice facility is the last stop on a very long, extremely rigorous training road for the astronaut candidate. Here, they use both reality and virtual reality to simulate using different tools. They learn how to work at a capacity that doesn't make them sweat. And they learn to manage their fluids, those going in, those coming out. There's a working space toilet in the mockup of the ISS. And potential astronauts, hooked up to monitoring equipment, with cameras and microphones and a dozen people close by, must prove that they can successfully use it before they launch. Can't risk any "stage fright" up there. To put it bluntly . . . they have to poop first. No go = no go.

Liquids in space are a really big deal because they'll float everywhere, including inside sensitive electronic equipment. It's such a big deal that most women in space choose to cycle off their periods, via hormonal regulation, for the duration of their time on the ISS. Of course NASA can't force that upon these women, but who the heck wants to mess with a tampon in addition to everything else?

As I mentioned, the astronauts learn how to work without sweating in a weightless environment. They do so in NASA's giant pool where, as in space, they're monitored with audio, an electrocardiogram, and sensors that measure oxygen consumption and carbon dioxide expiration. A typical American space suit is pressurized to 4.3 pounds per square inch (PSI). A Russian suit is pressurized to 5.2 (just their preference). The atmospheric pressure on Earth and aboard the ISS is about 14.7 PSI, in comparison. Each suit is plumbed with 100 percent oxygen, compared with about 21 percent on Earth. The 4.3 PSI is roughly equivalent to the air pressure at 32-33,000 feet above sea level, higher than Mount Everest. That's why the increased saturation of oxygen is required for the exertion of a space walk, a tense time in which every move is choreographed and rehearsed.

The physicians at Mission Control help the astronauts regulate their pace of work and have the authority to shut down the extravehicular activity (EVA) at any time if there is concern over astronaut safety. Whether a space walk is navigated to completion or aborted prematurely, it takes about two hours to equalize the pressure in the suits and to allow the astronauts to free themselves from them. It's analogous to a diver needing to decompress when rising from the depths of the sea, except in reverse. If either rushes the process, carbon dioxide (CO_2) can precipitate in the blood and cause the bends.

Depending on the type of mission, that recompression now typically happens while the astronaut "sits" in his suit just outside the space vehicle or in an airlock kind of room. On missions to the moon, or theoretically, missions to Mars, the suit would be left hanging outside the vehicle but plugged into it, like docking an iPhone on a tabletop charger. The astronaut, after equilibrating, would climb out the back of it, leaving the dusty space boots outside, where the particles couldn't float around and clog up the computers.

One of the Italian astronauts, Luca Parmitano, who we ran into while he was leading a tour for some visiting scientists, learned just how long that two hours can feel when he almost drowned in his space suit in 2013. There had been a water leak as the result of a clogged filter, and the moisture from his exhaled breath condensed inside the headpiece of his suit. He communicated to Mission Control that he could feel water at the back of his head. Then the liquid began to track around the side of his face toward his mouth and nose, like a living Saran Wrap. The EVA was immediately aborted, and his recompression initiated. The water filled his eyes, blinding him. He made his way back to the air lock by touch and by memory. The water filled his ears, deafening him. It filled his nose. It would've been like trying to breathe through a scuba mouthpiece while you have a water-filled face mask over your eyes and nose.

The moving film of water was centimeters away from tracking over his mouth, when his expedited recompression was complete, and he was able to open his suit and wipe the moisture from
his face. It was one of the closest calls for any EVA mishap and
was considered a high-visibility incident. His doctor on Earth
knew him so well, as they all do, that he could hear the fear in
Parmitano's voice, betraying his outward calm and discipline,
across thousands of miles of airless distance between them. That's
the kind of relationship they all develop and maintain for life. The
Italian was credited for his discipline by the Mishap Investigation
Board who wrote in their report that "EV2's [Parmitano's] calm
demeanor in the face of his helmet filling with water possibly
saved his life."

Many things are very different in space, including basic car-
diorespiratory physiology. In the absence of atmosphere and
gravity the chest expands, the diaphragm moves up within the
thorax, and there is a "globalization" of ventilation throughout all
the lung fields, as opposed to the ventilation of the apices (top of
the lungs) in our normal relaxed breathing on Earth. The shape of
the heart changes. People are less hungry and lose weight rapidly.
The pull of muscle on bones diminishes and degrades the calci-
um matrix. And the shape of the eyeball changes, enough so that
many astronauts return from the ISS permanently more farsight-
ed than they left Earth. It's unclear why that happens, but a pos-
tulated cause is the chronically high CO_2 environment aboard.

There are lithium-bed canister CO_2 scrubbers on board that
attempt to remove that natural physiologic byproduct. But the
current technology is limited by size and heat generation. Most
heat disbursement on Earth happens through convection, which
is why a gentle breeze makes a warm summer day more pleasant
or why a December wind makes the air feel much colder. With no
atmosphere in space, and only a miniscule breeze, getting rid of
heat is a challenge.

Those lithium-bed canisters also use power and materials and produce water. We've reached the natural boundary of

each of those variables, based upon our current physics, so the astronauts endure a higher level of CO_2 constantly. In fact, the delicate mixture of gasses on board would be significantly impacted by the administration of enriched oxygen to an ill astronaut. So much so, that after several hours of it, the ISS would have to be abandoned due to the fire potential created. So the decision to use oxygen as a treatment modality is a big deal and a group collaboration.

There is such a thing as space motion sickness, which gets treated with Phenergan just like it does on Earth. Even taste buds change in space, as the fluid in the tissues of the mouth shift and the taste buds at the back of the mouth engorge. Space workers spend a lot of time taste testing food in the food lab before they launch. But it's not uncommon for them to notice significant changes in flavor after a short time in space. Things that didn't taste bitter on Earth may be bitter on the ISS. In addition to the food that comes up on resupply rockets from the food lab, already about three years old when it arrives, there is a small experimental garden on the ISS where they are successfully growing some vegetables. It's actually easier to grow big vegetables in space than on Earth, and it's thought that it has something to do with freer gene expression in an extraterrestrial environment.

In addition to the aerospace cooks and docs, there are aerospace dentists and ophthalmologists and audiologists, mostly from UTMB, who screen candidates prior to deployment and surveil them for life as part of the Lifetime Study of Astronaut Health program. The full battery of astronaut screening tests and qualifications is not published, nor was it revealed to me in my inquiry, as an effort to prevent subversion or cheating. There are cardiac stress tests and echocardiograms, MRIs and ultrasounds, color vision tests, and the updating of vaccinations and dental fillings. There is first aid training and fire suppression. There are space vehicle puncture drills and a quick spin in the g-force centrifuge. Astronauts practice CPR and the transporting of an unconscious colleague to the CPR platform or Crew Medical Restraint System in one pod of the ISS.

We have no idea if CPR would work in space, in the absence of gravity, but we know that chest compressions can be done as long as both parties, victim and rescuer, are strapped in place. This was tested on a zero gravity flight where CPR was performed on a dummy for about twenty seconds. We also don't know how medications work with the fluid shifts, variable tissue perfusion, and changes in gastric absorption and liver metabolism.

We do know that it takes three to four hours to evacuate a sick or injured astronaut from the low earth orbit of the ISS, which circles the earth almost sixteen times per day. They would land in Kazakhstan. I ask Dr. Tarver how many times that's been done and he replies, "Zero. And we're trying to keep it zero."

It takes about twice that long, eight to twelve hours, for the crew to be capable of standing against gravity without assistance. They'll often need help getting out of the landing pod, into the waiting boat, helicopter, and jet that will take them all the way home to Houston. The whole process is about forty-eight hours. From the moon, it would take about seven days to bring someone urgently back. And there will be no evacuation from Mars. That's a one-way trip, if we ever make it.

Engineering and medical crews are set up to receive the astronauts in a number of facilities around the globe if necessary. There are ten NASA centers, each of which is equipped with a small clinic with a physician or mid-level provider (such as a nurse practitioner or physician assistant), a registered nurse or paramedic, and an administrative officer. There are also fully staffed fire departments in Florida, Texas, and New Mexico dedicated to NASA employees. During the return trip from the ISS, a prime landing site and a backup site are designated and actively staffed with robust rescue and air traffic control crews. During the shuttle program, at launch time, there were staff deployed at White Sands in New Mexico and at several overseas sites that were potential bail-out sites for the shuttle in the event of an aborted launch.

While there are so many things that are different in space, the rest of life is the same. One important development over the last decade or so is the advent of satellite-based cell phone communications. It used to be that if an astronaut wanted to speak to a family member, or vice versa, that the family had to come into Mission Control and be connected with their loved one over the same radio the controllers use to communicate. It was infrequent and not private. Now, an astronaut's husband can pick up his cell phone and call her up. A scientist's kids can text him, send emojis if they wish. There's Skype in space, too. There's Facebook and Instagram and Twitter and *The New York Times*.

While it's a benefit to be able to stay in touch with family on these long deployments, it also means that all the mundane parts of life we all deal with cannot be escaped, even if gravity can. If little Johnny gets a "D" on a test, his father or mother aboard the ISS must add that to their list of tasks that need attending. In other words, life goes on.

Except when it doesn't. One astronaut lost his mother while he was aboard. Most of the crews' families live in or around Houston, so every hurricane is intently watched both on the radar and from the window. The ISS passes overhead about every hour and a half. Which means that on board, the sun rises or sets every forty-five minutes. On my visit to Mission Control, I had hoped to be able to speak with the crew, but I came during their designated sleep time, and thus they could not be disturbed.

It's the physician in Mission Control who regulates the schedule, including time for experiments; three hours of weight-bearing, bone-strengthening exercise; and eight hours of sleep. There are enough experiments lined up to keep all six of the crew busy for twenty-four Earth hours per day for a full revolution of the sun. So, the doctors essentially become the guardians of sleep. They indicate to the crew when it's time to retire to their darkened, individualized sleeping pods. And then serve as a gentle vocal alarm clock eight hours later.

Even with all that careful planning, training, and attention, space is challenging. There are language barriers and cultural differences. There is fear and pressure and loneliness. There are the twin "big brothers" of the NASA machine and of social media. These men and women become ambassadors, diplomats for life. And that fishbowl can be hard to inhabit. With all the technology in their space suits, nothing insulates them from being elementally human.

There is a team of behavioral health specialists, psychiatrists and psychologists, who are present and available throughout selection, training, deployment, return to Earth, and continuing life after the mission. There is a private secure line from the ISS to a separate console in Mission Control by which an astronaut can speak freely regarding physical and mental health concerns. The families of the crew are also welcome to utilize medical services at the clinic on the Johnson Space Center campus.

There has been one astronaut who committed suicide and one rather well-known incident involving a woman who exhibited some behavioral disturbances upon her return. There are a few divorces and a little bit of alcohol dependence, though in lower proportion to the general population. No one has died in space, except in those catastrophic launch or reentry disasters at the outer atmosphere. The ones we all watched. But the first generation of astronauts is now in their eighties and several have passed away at the natural end of their lives. Given that the medical staff follows these folks for life, losing one of them is like losing a member of a very closely-knit family. Dr. Tarver mourns the same way we all do.

At the other end of the span of life, no one has been pregnant in space. It's doubtful that an embryo in utero would fare well in the g-forces associated with reentry. And, as far as we know, no one has had sex in space. That doesn't, however, mean that there's been no sperm.

Several petri dishes of semen were sent up in 2017 for a series of observations and tests. And knowing the anatomy, physiology, and psychology of the typical active, healthy, young-to-middle-aged male, I don't think those samples represent the first of the stuff to be in orbit. Even celibate priests who don't participate in masturbation still have unintentional nocturnal emissions. It's just biology. And I'm just curious. That's who I am.

Thankfully, as I pose the opening question to Dr. Tarver, "What happens when an astronaut ejaculates in space?" he has a sense of humor about it. A mellow laugh accompanies that calm, patient voice. That's just who he is.

He and his team take care of about fifty working astronauts at any given time, but those fifty people absorb most of the resources dedicated to the ten thousand or so employees at the Johnson Space Center in Clear Lake, Texas. The rest of the staff is made up of civil servants, private contractors, and security and healthcare workers. That number is down from the fifteen thousand employees at NASA's peak, prior to the closure of the space shuttle program and the general budget cuts that came out of the Great Recession.

Most NASA employees are office-based engineers and scientists whose jobs present no specific health risks outside those that are found in any occupational health setting, though there are several laboratories and hardware engineering environments that provide chemical exposure and radiation risks. There are aircraft routinely operating in the area, so NASA has a robust hearing conservation program. Because of the age of building construction at most NASA facilities, there is also an aggressive asbestos abatement program in place. Even given all that excitement, the most common injuries on the premises are of the slip-and-fall type.

In today's environment, given the frequency of workplace gun violence, active shooter drills are a regular part of planning and training at every NASA facility. There were two deaths, including the perpetrator, associated with a hostage situation and shooting at the space center's Building 44 in the Communication and Tracking Development Lab in 2007.

Given the demands and dangers of the job, it's reasonable to ask why anyone wants to be a part of it. The answer comes easily to Dr. Tarver. He and others like him get to be part of the most advanced, visionary, exciting research on the planet. When he talks about Mars research, it's not just about climate change and über-long-distance travel and sustainability. What we learn about medication shelf life and medication preservation, as we try to develop things that will last beyond the duration of the trip, can be applied to terrestrial pharmaceuticals. Remotely controlled surgical robots and the surgical suite of the future that could enable a doctor on Earth to remove a gallbladder on Mars are already being put to use in operating rooms around the world.

We're learning more about radiation and its carcinogenic effects. We're finding new ways of purifying water, of utilizing solar energy, and of growing things more efficiently. By following the astronauts long-term, we're learning more about the preservation of bone density and the reduction of atherosclerosis. All of it is impactful.

On top of that, though, and far more important, is the opportunity the medical crew gets to form an indelible bond with some of the most amazing men and women on Earth. Even when they're off it.

"Wild Oglalas"

Viral social media and flash-in-the-pan emergencies
Standing Rock Sioux Reservation,
North and South Dakota. Spring.

There's no one standing here with me. No one at all. Not even
a highway patrol officer or a game warden out to see what I'm
up to. Though I cross a blue "U.S. Govt Property" sign, I apparently don't trigger any alarms when I walk through the gap in
the triple-strand barbed wire fence and venture onto the protest
grounds. There are no alarms, no guards, no National Guards-
men. No helicopter or drone buzzing me. No buried seismo-
graph, apparently. And no visible pipeline, not even the slightest
hint of where one might be buried.

I look for it in earnest. I'm not trespassing for naught, though
I'm walking this field mostly to capture the spirit, not to find that
buried conduit. I know it's here. It's the reason the nation came
to know this place for a flash-in-the-pan moment in 2016. It's the
reason the celebrities came out for a minute, then quickly retreated to the warmth of California. It's the reason the media, both
liberal and conservative, came out in droves, though for the most
part they rented hotel rooms in nearby towns instead of endur-
ing the brutal North Dakota winter in a tent. Social media feeds

buzzed with chanted slogans. But now I stand here at Standing Rock, alone.

All those tweets and posts about "I stand with Standing Rock" have grown silent, as has the enormous boring machine that dropped the now-functioning Dakota Access Pipeline (DAPL) under the Missouri River. The construction work is finished. Armchair protestors, mouse in hand, have moved on to other topics more current. Clickbait clickers, smartphone in hand, are busy trumpeting some other cause, joining some other bandwagon. They packed up their virtual cares and left while the Native American protestors were still reinforcing their tents and yurts for a North Dakota winter.

If they really stood with Standing Rock, they'd stand with the women here. They'd speak out against domestic violence and sexual predation on the reservation. If they really stood with Standing Rock, they'd donate to diabetes research and write a check to the local Indian Health Service clinic. They'd fund an addressing campaign so that ambulances have an easier time responding to 911 calls and disenfranchised Native Americans could have a physical address to put on a voter registration form. If they really stood with Standing Rock, they'd come here themselves to North Dakota. And they'd come prepared for the weather.

They'd stop by here and then they'd drive three and a half hours north and west, up into the Bakken oil field, following the 135-year-old train tracks. They would watch thousands of tanker cars of crude oil rock along a rickety, underfunded, aging rail system. Those who care would watch some twenty-five-year-old kid, who just got his Commercial Driver's License last week, try to back a loaded double trailer full of oil along the Little Missouri River and they'd realize why a pipeline is necessary, even if they disagreed with how and where it was built. If they cared, they'd research the permitting process for the DAPL, the barriers to access to survey and environmental research data, and the differences between Obama and Trump administration policies.

A quick survey of my own friends' Facebook posts reveals that none of them have posted anything about Standing Rock since 2016, even though the legal battles surrounding the relationship between Energy Transfer Partners, the federal government, and the sovereign tribe still persist today.

If people took the time to come here, they would stand on the bridge crossing the Cannonball River where it feeds into Lake Oahe (oh-wah-hee) and realize that they're not on Standing Rock Sioux sovereign territory. The protest grounds are on a tiny chunk of US Army Corps land bordered to the south by Standing Rock and to the north by private ranch land. And on that bridge, people would realize there is more to the story than what they saw on Facebook. Then they would ask questions. But people aren't asking questions anymore. They're gone. They've forgotten.

When I came to Standing Rock, I came from the west and the south. The protest grounds are in North Dakota. But that particular Sioux reservation spans both North and South Dakota. It's huge. And beautiful. And hard. And it represents a fraction of the land the Sioux used to inhabit. The eastern border of the reservation here is the Missouri River, which, in this part of the country, widens into Lake Oahe. Lake Oahe starts just south of the city of Mandan, North Dakota, and is about half as wide there as the Hudson River at Albany, twice as wide as the Rio Grande. The lake's southern terminus is the dam at Pierre (pronounced "peer"), South Dakota's capital.

The Missouri is not an insignificant waterway. The "Mighty Mo" headwaters deep in western Montana from Brower's Spring, near the Continental Divide and 9,100 feet above the sea, on Mount Jefferson. The "Big Muddy" drains more than half a million square miles, touching ten US states and two Canadian provinces that are remarkably sparsely inhabited. The region is certainly more heavily populated than it was twelve thousand years ago when Indigenous folks were known to be using the 2,300 miles of the Missouri's water for life and food and transportation. The Standing Rock Sioux are one of more than ten Native American tribes that have depended on and loved the Pekita-noui for a hundred generations, all the way down to its confluence with the Mississippi, where it becomes the world's fourth-longest waterway.

There are well over a hundred modern bridges that cross the Mighty Mo. About nine of those are in North Dakota. I can't see any of them from where I'm standing. I'm on top of a small, two-lane bridge over the Cannonball River, where it drains into the Missouri.

To the south is a little rise that obscures my view of Highway 1806 as it continues down through the Sioux Reservation and eventually links up with other roads that go to Pierre. To the west is a gentle, wide ravine that's been slowly cut by the Cannonball as it drains the spring runoff of the higher elevations down into the Missouri. To the north, new pavement winds lazily toward Fort Rice and Mandan and Canada. I drove all of the road I can currently see and a dozen miles in every direction, looking for the protest grounds. My tires warmed this very bridge half a dozen times before I finally stopped at a gas station in town and asked someone to pinpoint the location on my map. I thought surely there would be some signs of what had gone on here. But the years and the winters have passed and all but erased the footprints.

Now as I turn to the east and face the serpentine course of brown water, a couple hundred yards from the Missouri itself, I'm turning my face away from the wind. That wind is cold today, but not bitterly so. It's dry, crispy out.

I pull my knit cap over my head and tuck my hands into lightweight neoprene gloves. The wind stays at my back as I descend from the low bridge and approach a barbed-wire ranch fence. There's a gap in it without a gate, just about large enough to fit a big truck. On the left-hand side, there's a small blue sign, one-quarter the size of a license plate. It declares the large field in front of me to be US Government property.

A glance in all directions helps me confirm that I'm alone: no people, no livestock, no cameras. There's only the field. Now that I'm standing on the prairie itself, I feel small in comparison to the brown grasses, drying in the cold sun. I am shorter than the tall thistles and brambles. They must make it challenging to walk here in their full summer bloom. Right now, they resemble clusters of tall toothpicks with big cotton balls on their tops. Everything is brown and hard, even the dirt.

I start to walk, slowly, listening for the voices that once rallied here, feeling for the tension this ground must have absorbed. I can tell that I'm on the remnant of a de facto road, and I follow it as it rounds into a wide horseshoe, big enough to fit a football field along its interior. It seems to dip into the protest ground and then ascend back up to the road surface, maybe half a mile north of where I parked. Every once in a while there's the hint of a foot-path branching off this main track.

I don't see the marks of tents or tepees or fire pits. Summers of growth have obscured those. I can't see the open-pit latrines the protestors used. They were filled in by the National Guard. I can't see the hundreds of abandoned propane tanks and gas cans that were left behind. The state police disposed of those. I can't see the tracks of bulldozers that cleared more than twenty roll-off dumpsters worth of detritus when the site was vacated.

All I see is a dry flood plain, ground that is often underwater after the spring thaw, ground that was certainly underwater after the unusually high snowfall of the winter of 2016. In March this field becomes untenable, and whatever is on it floats east and into the rapid waters of the Missouri, the very water this protest was supposed to be protecting. It's the same water that carried a foul odor in April when the spring thaw came. A rancher alerted the sheriff of Morton County, who had been expecting the smell.

A quick search upstream by law enforcement officers revealed the body of an occupier who had disappeared. He was presumed to have drowned when he failed to return to the encampment.

The dead man was one of two people who lost their lives, the other having had a fatal heart attack. Given the length of the occupation, the depth of passionate feelings, and the volume of people who came in contact with the Oceti Sakowin "Rosebud" camp, the fatal toll could easily have been higher.

In the end, it took a toll of another type, one that's still visible in the cautious faces of law enforcement officers and paramedics around town. More so than any other place, when I came here with pen in hand, the metaphorical gates began to come down. At first meeting, people lump me into the category of "media." And after the catastrophic influence of our overwhelming traditional and nontraditional media presence for two-thirds of a year, these folks are understandably skittish at the sight of my notebook.

I did my best to talk to the emergency responders and security from the camp, to the municipal police department, local fire department, both area ambulance providers, the state health department, and the hospital in Bismarck, but I was often funneled into the official channels of canned response and tight lips. Especially over the phone. That's part of why I came here in person, not to make a statement or push an agenda but simply to understand what it was like on the ground.

The first surprise was that I couldn't find it. Though the name actually denotes the Sioux tribe, Oceti Sakowin became the colloquial name for the protest grounds and is now listed on Google Maps. So is the Backwater Bridge, another little piece of elevated roadway here that gained notoriety on November 20, 2016, when snow and ice already covered the road and dusted the backs of the cattle munching hay on ranches nearby. Even so, it's hard to spot.

Now, I'm standing on it, and as I walk, I catalogue the few items I find left behind after the month-long cleanup and the intervening seasons. Spread out over the acres, I come across two wool socks of different colors and different sizes. There's a hoodie sweatshirt, a length of rope, two broken tent poles, and a deck of playing cards that are blown out into a wide circle by the North

Dakota wind. I find one beer can, stomped flat, and what looks like a piece of shelving from a convenience store.

The shelf has silver duct tape adhered to the front edge and labels written in red Sharpie: tomato soup, tomato sauces and pastes, diced tomatoes. This then, must've been the commissary. The high salt content in each of those cans probably kept them from freezing, at least until winter was at its coldest. The campers organized, as many "Occupy" groups do. Within the protest grounds they set up the commissary, a community kitchen, a fuel station, a medical yurt, an entertainment area, a direction post, a law office, a command center, and a library. There was a main road with spur routes and organized tent sites.

In the beginning, occupiers shat in buckets and either buried their stool at the fringes of the protest grounds or emptied their buckets into the Cannonball River. As the population swelled, they added compost toilets and dug trench latrines, which eventually also leeched into the Missouri River. Their efforts at sanitation were not robust enough to prevent more than two hundred ambulance rides for gastrointestinal distress and other infectious illnesses.

I survey the field, so still except for the waving of dead thistles, and in my mind I can superimpose their grid on the brittle dirt. Slowly, something appears out of the fog of my fantasy, something white. Small. It's off in the distance, on a stick. It must be some sort of signage. A marker. It's probably fifty yards from me. Then I see another, and another. Now that they're in my vision, I can't believe I didn't see them before. In this brown-on-brown landscape under a gloomy sky they now stick out like beacons, and before I know it I'm walking toward them.

"Maybe this is the pipeline," I think. "Maybe these are some sort of 'Call Before You Dig,' or 'Buried Conduit,' or hazmat markers."

It's hard to gain perspective here, and I can't tell how far away they are. I reach the first one faster than I anticipated, and as I crunch through the dead grass toward it I realize it's not sturdy enough or permanent enough to be an official marker. Getting close, I can see that it's plain white, the size of an 8 ½" x 11" sheet of paper, turned sideways in landscape view.

That's exactly what it is, a piece of printed paper, thickly laminated and stapled to a wooden dowel stuck in the ground. Standing in front of it, it rises to mid-thigh. And it says, "Direction Post." I stare at it for a moment and then lift my eyes, scanning behind me toward the road and beside me to the flanking bluffs. "Holy shit!" I say to the wind.

It's a piece of ephemera that not only survived the abandonment of the camp, the final clearing by the law enforcement team, but also a brutally cold, incessantly windy North Dakota winter. It also survived the rise and fall of a movement. It stands here in defiance of the floodwaters, as if waiting to point any stragglers toward another interest, toward some other occupation. Apparently it's been effective as a sign, directing everyone away from here. Because, with another look around, I'm still devastatingly alone.

Now, I have to know what the other two white markers say. I can't feel the cold or the wind anymore as I stumble over the uneven ground toward them. Number two says, "Wild Oglalas." I push on toward sign number three, the most pristine of them. It's the furthest from the road, from the bridge, from where my vehicle sits alone waiting for me. And it's exactly why I came here. My steps slow as I approach it.

"You gotta be fucking kidding me," I say softly. I get to the sign, 8½" x 11" on a stick, defying the wind. I stand with my feet shoulder width apart and my hands on my hips, my jaw lowered, and mouth open. I start to smile. I turn in a circle and start to laugh.

"You gotta be fucking kidding me!"

A covey of partridges lifts out of the low trees along the water, startled by my shouts of incredulity and my loony laughter. I look down at it again and I'm overcome with emotion, somber now. My heart twists in my chest and my feet quiet under me. There are two words printed on this sign. And, reading them, I know I've found what I came here to find. I found my people.

MEDICAL

(Oceti)

This was the clinic outpost, where medical folks from the Sioux reservation and other Native nations around the country felt called to action and did their best to care for the people they believed in. I'm sure it wasn't easy.

I decide to commit my second crime of the day. In one hard swipe, I rip the sign off the post it was so carefully stapled to. And I start the long walk back to the road. On the off chance that a deputy or a patrolman is waiting for me at my vehicle with a trespassing summons, I tuck the sign under my shirt, under my vest and my coat, against my skin. It sits there, cold against my stomach for a few moments until it warms with the effort of my walking.

I'm ruminative on the walk back, feeling colder as I head into the wind. I arrive at the road, at the Cannonball Bridge, itself now heavy with the weight of history. And I see that there's no one waiting for me. No sheriff's deputy. No highway patrol. Still no National Guard or US Marshals or border patrol. No rancher stopped to see if I was okay. No Native American stopped to see what I was doing. No one cares that I'm here, standing on the place where people once "stood with Standing Rock."

I pull back up onto Highway 1806 and the fresh blacktop, and I head into Mandan to talk to a man who spent a year caring about who set foot there. I don't tell him about my lawlessness today, my trespass and my petty theft.

I first meet Morton County Sheriff Kirchmeier at the city hall building, home to a shared office space for Morton County Sheriff Department and the City of Mandan Police Department. The courthouse and the jail are here, along with other municipal offices like the tax assessor and the building inspector.

The fire department is down the road, and the Metro Area Ambulance Service is headquartered in Bismarck, across the river, with substations throughout the county. I wait politely on the street side of a bulletproof glass window, which separates the lobby from an open office of administrative staff, mostly women. I overhear the goings-on of a couple locals, elderly men, who came to complain about some small-town thing or another.

After a dozen or more minutes, a large, relaxed man with a sidearm displaces a waft of air as he enters the lobby. He takes my hand in a shake that involves my whole arm. His hand is big enough to completely engulf mine. He gazes a foot or more down at me and listens patiently as I explain why I'm here. He can't talk now. He's headed out soon and he wants the public information officer (PIO) to join our conversation. He invites me to a graduation. Several agencies around the state are swearing in new officers today, and he invites me to watch the ceremony. He promises to sit with me afterwards and answer my questions.

A couple hours later, on a dizzyingly bright and brisk afternoon, I head to the North Dakota Heritage Center in Bismarck. It's an impressive building, part auditorium, part state museum. Lots of natural light for the long, dark winter filters in through high glass walls. As a hundred booney hats file out of the building, I get a call from the PIO, and she tells me where I can join them. We sit around the corner from the main entrance in an alcove of stained concrete and glass and stainless-steel beams.

At a small table with fluorescent plastic chairs that seem frighteningly small for a human of his size, the three of us sit down. As I expect, the PIO is friendly, competent, engaging, informative, and professional. She's brought some stats and maps and timelines for reference. She gives me a list of verification websites that were created to try and get ahead of the misinformation train. They posted videos of their own from body cameras and dash cams and media footage. They created bulletins called "By the Numbers" and "Know the Truth." The commanders never fully caught up, nor got ahead of the locomotive of deception that picked up speed as it barreled through Morton County. But they did their best.

It didn't start out that way. Day One wasn't like the end, or like the middle, of the occupation. It seldom is in these extended protests. Mr. Kirchmeier was there for Day One, when the protestors numbered one, and when only he and his deputies were around. Soon though, the state highway patrol, the rural volunteer fire department, and the two area ambulance services (including Standing Rock Ambulance) were present. It would be a long time before they had enough help. In the end, there was the National Guard, the North Dakota Department of Health, EMTs, paramedics on rotation from around the state, Bureau of Criminal Investigation, warrant officers, parole and probation officers, ND Highway Patrol troopers, city cops on overtime, and sheriffs from every jurisdiction.

The area ranchers themselves, decades into growing the barley and canola and wheat of the Midwest, formed their own loose militia to help each other safeguard their property. Officially, they were encouraged to call 911, but North Dakota has a version of stand-your-ground law and a decidedly self-sufficient population. They created a farmers' phone tree. They helped each other patrol their fence lines, some of which were cut by demonstrators. They helped round up loose livestock, some of which were lost in the chaos. They loaned each other hay when bales were stolen.

In a tense moment, a group of water protectors encircled a rancher while he was on his tractor, plowing a field for the coming winter. They were on horseback and they stopped his forward progress. They rode around and around him in circles, flags waving on horse-mounted guidons like an old western cavalry scene. The rancher eventually dismounted from the cab holding a 12-gauge shotgun loaded with birdshot. The scene ended there, luckily with no one injured.

Conspicuously lacking at Oceti Sakowin was a federal presence. The DAPL is a federal pipeline, on federal property (Army Corps of Engineers), abutting a federal Indian reservation, but despite repeated requests for help under the Obama administration, no federal officers were sent to assist.

In the first four months, virtually every Morton County employee was on duty for some part of a day, every day of the week, without respite. For the 234 days of the encampment, no deputy left town and they were all working fourteen- to sixteen-hour days, sometimes longer. When the burden began to show, they organized a two-week-on/one-day-off rotation, though Sheriff Kirchmeier rarely took one. He was the incident commander from the outset. He took it from a span of control by two or three people, through the escalation of response infrastructure, to all the moments of high tension and high press, through the de-escalation, removal, cleanup, and the termination of command.

In the beginning, he was the PIO, trying to field media calls, manage social platforms, and make statements. After six months, he asked for a PIO and ended up with five, including the woman sitting across from me. She came to Mandan from the North Dakota Association of Counties and was there when a Change. org petition for Kirchmeier's removal from office gained 113,000 signatures. There were strong opinions from around the world about the use of force at the encampment during some of the most critical, and highly visible, moments.

The public information officer and her colleagues became the liaison for attorneys from the American Civil Liberties Union (ACLU) who came to Morton County to surveil the tactics of law enforcement officers, watchful for violations of the US Constitution and the infringement of civil rights. In the years since, there have been new lawsuits from the ACLU regarding training and preparations for potential anticipated protests regarding the Keystone XL Pipeline or the expansion of the Dakota Access Pipeline.

As group occupation protests go, Standing Rock has one of the longest tenures of any. It lasted 234 days. In comparison, Occupy Wall Street lasted fifty-nine days, concluding in November 2011, long before the New York winter (far milder than a North Dakota winter) set in. The 504 Sit-in of 1977, which helped push lawmakers toward securing rights and access for Americans with disabilities, lasted twenty-six days. Colin Kaepernick silently protested for fourteen Sundays until his option went unclaimed after he became a free agent in 2017.

Sheriff Kirchmeier makes it clear to me that from Day One, his highest priority was the safety of everyone present: his officers, the pipeline workers, county employees, the media, local ranchers, the protestors, and his own family. No one could have predicted the size or the duration of the occupation, which made it a challenge to allocate resources appropriately. For the most part, the encampment remained peaceful, vocal, and joyful, with traditional singing and drumming every day. As an illustration of that, the first water protectors raised their voices and raised their signs on April 1, but there wasn't an arrest from the site until August 10, four months later.

Kirchmeier begins to walk me through that almost-year of his life. He tells me about the railroad incident. A rail-mounted work convoy was making its way toward the construction and staging area, when occupiers stood on the tracks to stop it. In a frightening escalation, they pushed a pickup truck loaded with fuel in front of the stopped locomotive on the tracks. They laid a wick and moved behind it. Then they lit it. A highway patrolman ran to the truck and pulled out the burning wick before the flames could ignite it. It could have been much worse.

The power of a protest lies in the ability to disrupt. Disruption draws attention. Attention prompts conversation. Where many demonstrations flounder is in their inability to set and maintain a narrative, as happened at Occupy Wall Street. But even when the message is lost or evolves, disruption remains.

There is a small cluster of houses just north on Highway 1806 with less than a dozen people who live there full-time, year-round. Partway through the occupation a roadblock was placed on the highway, on the only road to their homes. It was a serpentine course of Jersey barriers that folks had to navigate every day as they came and went about their normal lives. They drove through it, every morning and every evening, for more than six months. They were required to present a valid ID, every time. Once, an eighteen-wheel delivery truck underestimated his length and got wedged in the barricade, stalling traffic in either direction for hours. There is a casino on the reservation and many of its workers live in Mandan. They also had to pass through the check-point twice a day. To take a different route might require an hour's worth of out-of-the-way travel in each direction. It was because Highway 1806 was so vital that the protestors chose it. It had the ability to disrupt.

Protestors and media were not permitted through the road-block, so they came from the south, from Standing Rock. The Oceti Sakowin camp was on federal, non-reservation land but the majority of the media were on the reservation itself.

I speak with a man who lives in that set of houses between the roadblock and the camp. Once the National Guard set up, his daily life changed. There are two public facilities along Highway 1806, on the Missouri River, that were natural strategic choices to put up a field office. The Fort Rice Recreation Area campsite, with two vault toilets and eight RV sites, became a deployment home for the troops, and they erected living tents, a field hospital, a mess hall, flatbed latrines and shower houses, a fuel depot, and a communications center. Gas-powered generators fired more than two hundred spotlights.

"It looked like a city," the old man tells me. His dog winds the leash around and around his legs while we talk. She's a big, hairy mutt of some sort that looks part Bernese Mountain Dog, part Labrador Retriever, part industrial kitchen mop. She's untrained. Her owner is an elderly fellow, and as he bobs and weaves, repeatedly unwinding himself from the rope, and has his arms nearly pulled from their sockets by his hyperactive dog, the paramedic in me is waiting for him to fall on his ass.

I meet him at the other Fort Rice facility, the boat launch. He points out his house to me and I have a direct line of sight to it. It's only a couple hundred yards away. This boat launch became the "intake" facility, the processing center for anyone arrested at the protest grounds. There is a little parking lot, a ramp for small craft to launch on the Missouri, and another set of two-vault toilets. This was where people in custody had their fingerprinting and photographing done, and where they waited in warm tents or warm trucks to be taken into Mandan or Bismarck.

In the beginning, there wasn't a need for an intake area. There just weren't any arrests. Under Barack Obama, after an emergency injunction, construction on the DAPL was paused while the construction permit was adjudicated. So both parties were simply waiting on the results. The protestors used that time to raise awareness and push for a fair, timely assessment of the potential impact of the pipeline (and of the potential for river contamination) on sacred sites, cemeteries, and medicinal plants in the area, among other things.

In November 2016, North and South Dakota voted Republican in a presidential election that saw Donald Trump defeat Hillary Clinton by 30 percent or more in both states. Native Americans at Standing Rock and on other reservations typically vote Democrat. But in 2016, many, many voters decided to sit out the election, dissatisfied with both candidates, disillusioned with a government that has repeatedly violated treaties with their sovereign nations, and disenfranchised by voter ID requirements —the absence of a physical address with which to register—and a lack of transportation to carry them long distances to a paucity of polling places.

In a high turnout year, 47 percent of residents of Sioux County, North Dakota, came to the polls. And a month before the 2018 mid-term election, new voter ID laws were enacted that turned away a fair number of those who had made the trek to cast their vote. Barack Obama won their vote overwhelmingly in 2012, while Hillary prevailed by a much smaller margin in 2016. The socioeconomic disparity between White Republican voters in North Dakota whose jobs are anchored by agriculture, the military, and the oil field at 2–3 percent unemployment, and Native American Democratic voters on reservation lands, where the unemployment rate can be up to 30 percent, is vast. And the history of racism in the Midwest is deep and often overlooked.

The overwhelming majority of the 1,172 miles of pipe are laid into ground that was taken, either by consent and negotiation or by eminent domain lawsuit, from private lands. Ninety-nine percent of land owners consented to a buyout, including over five hundred parcels and $189 million in "just compensation" for a pipe that is 2.5 feet in diameter with a 50-foot easement. None of the pipe runs under reservation land and no just compensation was provided to the tribe.

Donald Trump took office in early 2017, and within four days issued a presidential memorandum that essentially ended ongoing legal, cultural, and environmental discussion, granted the easement, and enabled the resumption of construction on the Dakota Access Pipeline. It was only then that the occupiers were "officially" trespassing. It's worth noting that Donald Trump was an investor in Energy Transfer Partners, the company that, along with minor partners like Phillips 66 and Marathon Petroleum, built the pipeline. He took in more than $100,000 from their CEO for his 2016 presidential campaign.

Soon after taking office, Mr. Trump sent federal officers to the protest grounds in the form of border patrol agents. The site of the Oceti Sakowin encampment is about two hundred miles from the border, in as straight a line as the roads can provide. A reasonable "crow flies" estimate, or air-travel estimate as it's more clearly defined, would still probably be about 190 miles from what is the longest two-country border in the world.

The border patrol has a jurisdiction that extends inland from the United States' terrestrial and maritime borders by one hundred miles, which means that the states of Delaware, Massachusetts, New Jersey, Florida, Maine, New Hampshire, Vermont, Hawaii, Rhode Island, and most of New York are within USBP authority. Nine of the ten largest cities in the United States are within one hundred miles of a coast or a border, including New York City, Chicago, Los Angeles, Houston, Seattle, Philadelphia, Phoenix, both Portlands, and all of Silicon Valley.

Mandan, North Dakota, is not one of those nine cities. Nor is it on a coast. It is about 160 miles south of the 49th parallel and, traditionally, beyond the traditional reach of the USBP. Those officers in green and white came late to the party at Standing Rock and they missed Backwater Bridge.

The roadblock on Highway 1806 sat near the Backwater Bridge and sat between the water protectors and almost everything else. To the north were casino patrons who were no longer spending money on the cards and the dice. To the north was the hospital that would see a sudden spike in visitorship in 2016 and 2017. Also to the north of the bridge were all the patrol cars, cruisers, radio infrastructure, lethal and non-lethal weapons, and ammunition that had become part of the law enforcement presence at the encampment.

• • •

As early twilight fell, snow sat quiescent on the prairie, piled up by the plow along the road's edge. That white surface began to reflect light, first flashlights and headlamps, then spotlights raised above diesel generators, then the orange-yellow of flames. Ten thousand protestors had come to North Dakota by that time, from as near as South Dakota and as far as Australia. And they set their sights on dismantling the roadblock, which they saw as economic retaliation against the Standing Rock tribe.

They were more than three thousand strong, standing across the Jersey barriers and the concertina wire from about fifty police officers. Campers set fire to vehicles near the roadblock and officers donned riot gear over their winter coats and balaclavas. Verbal warnings were sent out over patrol car PAs and bullhorns. Protestors were told to keep their distance.

A Long Range Acoustic Device and pepper spray were of little effect. The pepper spray blew back into the faces of the officers. The local volunteer fire department attempted to douse the burning cars with the water supply they had in the tank. They were outmatched by the volume of fire. Protestors began to advance on the officers. Burning frisbees and flaming paper airplanes soared toward the police and landed among them. Rolled up lengths of barbed wire were made into frisbees and tossed at the officers. A rock was thrown with a slingshot and an officer went to the ground, hit in the head hard enough to knock him unconscious despite his helmet.

A group of men began to dismantle the guardrail along the highway. They unscrewed the bolts and used their slingshots to fire them at the officers. Still, the warnings were sent. Professional restraint kept weapons holstered and feet planted. Protestors were instructed to retreat behind the line of demarcation at the roadblock.

The group of three thousand spread out and began to move north in a wide arc, outflanking the smaller uniformed group. If they succeeded in going around the cops, they would have access to weapons and ammunition and vehicles. The noisy but peaceful protest was bound to take a deadly turn. Still the cars burned. Still the people advanced. At some point, law enforcement utilized the fire hoses to push the mass backward.

It worked. It was cold. The group retreated. No shots were fired. No one died. No cars exploded as they burned. But many people became hypothermic and a couple dozen people were taken to the hospital for blunt-force traumatic injuries. The officer who had taken a lug nut to the forehead and three of his partners were also transported.

Once that moment de-escalated and both teams had debriefed amongst themselves, videos of the fire hoses went worldwide viral. In fact, the first time I heard about Standing Rock was in Facebook posts that decried, "Police use water cannons on Native Americans on Thanksgiving Day."

Before I knew anything about what was being protested and why, I wondered about the medics, the folks thrust in to care for a hundred hypothermic people. It was that image that prompted me to drive here, later, to see for myself. And it was nothing like I pictured.

My next surprise was to find that the contested water is a man-made reservoir. There's a dam at the south end that artificially broadens the course of the Mighty Mo from just north of Pierre up to Mandan and Bismarck. The hydroelectric plant there provides power for a huge chunk of the north-central United States, including the reservation, and includes high-tension wires that run over Lake Oahe. Construction on the dam started in 1948 and the first kilowatts were generated in 1962 when President Kennedy, in attendance, said, "Water is our most precious asset, and its potential uses are so many and so vital that they are frequently in conflict."

As one of six dams on the mainstream Missouri, Oahe Dam provides agricultural irrigation, flood control, fishing, recreation, and navigation that would not otherwise exist. Without it, a portion of the Midwest that is currently arable farmland would be underwater in the spring, and the rest would be dark at night.

However, under that water right now are 460,000 acres of Native American land that were seized and inundated in the late 1940s under the Pick-Sloan Plan. The dam projects of the Pick-Sloan project, and the post-war industrialization of agriculture, submerged hundreds of communities across the west, both Native and non-Native, but none so vastly as the Oahe Dam. Also submerged at Lake Oahe are seven other pipelines, already transporting crude oil.

My first instinct when I first saw the dam was to ponder why people would be so incensed about a theoretical threat to a waterway that was already significantly altered and developed more than half a century ago. I saw the lake as artificial and the threat of contamination as miniscule. Once I knew a bit more of the antecedent history, I could appreciate the passion of the Standing Rock Sioux toward a waterway that had previously been a contested and painful part of their heritage.

And that's just the thing. There's nuance. There's perspective. There's history. There is family and poverty and the loss of a way of life that has dwindled slowly away. Native tribes in North America have been forced around the continent, their "homeland" fluid. Many tribes have had little control over where they land and little permanency of place.

While today's Standing Rock reservation boundaries weren't drawn by anyone reading this book, they are still encroached upon by several industries that support the current United States as a whole, the Midwest as a region, and the Sioux as a tribe. It's impossible to read about these things in 140 characters. The wrinkles of worry on a face aren't discernable in a grainy YouTube video. Facebook cannot provide a fair assessment of the situation. And this is too complicated a picture for Instagram. And that's just the point. I do not possess the whole picture. And I cannot possibly convey it in one chapter. There have been books and scholarly papers written about these same contested lands every decade, and more to come, I hope.

In terms of statute alone, the resistance to the construction of the Dakota Access Pipeline concerned the Fort Laramie Treaties of 1851, 1868, and 1876, the Supremacy Clause of the Constitution, the National Historic Preservation Act, the Clean Water Act, the Indian Removal Act of 1830, the Indian Appropriations Act, The Dawes Act, the Indian Reorganization Act, the 1944 Flood Control Act, the National Environmental Preservation Act, the Religious Freedom Restoration Act, the Standing Rock Tribal Code of Justice, the Freedom of Information Act, and the First, Second, Fourth, Fifth, Eighth, Tenth, Eleventh, and Fifteenth Amendments.

It's the kind of moment in history that requires thoughtful contemplation and factual, historically accurate, open-minded discussion. But ever more these days, there's a degradation of integrity in favor of expediency. With our rapid pace of self-publication and the quick digestion of Snapchat images, the iron is perpetually hot. New people strike at it every day. Sometimes every hour. That can be deadly. And through all of that, there are men and women on the ground fulfilling their call to duty, irrespective of their political opinions about the matter at hand. Police officers, firefighters, EMTs, nurses, physicians, pilots, and dispatchers put themselves in harm's way and are, at best, under-recognized for it, and, at worst, threatened with violence, rape, and death by internet trolls. That's part of why most of them wouldn't talk to me when I came here.

When the final two or three dozen most stalwart trespassers were removed on February 23, 2017, Morton County brought in large buses to transport them. Protestors boarded them, for the most part, peacefully. Anyone who left voluntarily was provided a hotel room and a bus ticket to anywhere in the Lower 48. There were a few who resisted arrest and made for good footage on network news, but they were a small minority.

In those final moments, the narrative, again, diverged. Footage shows the camp on fire. Half the news channels and a large portion of social media feeds made it seem as though the police were "burning tepees and knifing tents." The other half made it sound like the protestors burned the tepees as a sacred ceremony. It was neither, really.

It was the last gasp of disruption. It was performance. And it was dangerous with the propane tanks and the wind. Two kids were badly burned, one teenage girl and one young boy. They were some of the last patients out of several hundred who were transported by either Metro Area Ambulance Service or Standing Rock Ambulance. Both survived. But their story was not broadly told.

There is no burn center in North or South Dakota, so they were sent to other hospitals, probably in Colorado or Minnesota. No one would tell me. Those two young people, like the detritus of the Oceti Sakowin camp, were scattered to the wind, just like the deck of cards I found there. They were Oglalas in the truest sense. In Lakota, Oglala means "to scatter one's own." For a little while at Standing Rock, everything was scattered, and everything was wild.

A Night in South Valley

"They can always hurt you more."
—Samuel Shem. The House of God
Las Cruces, New Mexico. Summer. A long time ago.

I remember the first one who hurt me. It was a hot August night and I was eighteen. I was driving a Nissan Maxima, the old boxy one with the sunroof and the number pad on the door.

I had already felt the call of duty. That irrepressible thing in me that's kept me at it all this miserable time, all this wonderful time. I dutifully wore that pager on my right hip all the time. And it had gone off with that familiar jolting, blaring, chirping sound. It was a sound that would subsequently roust me from my bed for another thirteen years. That night was near the beginning of those years. And I hadn't yet had a dead one.

I knew as much as I could about what I was getting into. I'd prepared with a bit of book learning and a bit of the storytelling. A lot of the downtime spent in the firehouse centers around stories. The old ones speak of the days of old and the young ones speak of last week. It's part of how a firefighter becomes a firefighter, in every sense, right down to the steel-toed stance and its stoicism. I didn't yet have any stories of my own to tell.

Crackle . . . chirp . . . static . . .

"Mesilla Fire, mutual aid . . .
2100 *some little road* in South Valley
For a diabetic problem."
Squelch . . .

As I rolled out of bed, where I'd not yet been asleep, and stepped into the low-key uniform I always, always, kept with me, sweating already on that hot, still night along the Rio Grande, I wondered why the neighboring department would need mutual aid. Why would they need additional manpower on what seemed like a mundane and routine EMS call? I keyed up:

Crackle . . . squelch . . .
"Mesilla 8-4 en route."
"Copy Mesilla 8-4."
[pause]
"Mesilla 4-5 en route."
"Copy Mesilla 4-5."

That was Chad. When he marked en route, as he very nearly always did, I knew I wasn't going alone. Other firefighters followed us by a few minutes, and I knew from the distance between our houses that I'd have about a minute and a half on Chad. I opened the sunroof on the Maxima and stuck my "Kojak light" (a magnetic, egg-shaped, red-revolving beacon) on the roof. Flashers on, foot on the floor. Blast through the pecan orchards and onto some dusty little road, where a cacophony of flashing lights disoriented me, as they did in the early days.

It was a single-wide trailer with a chain-link fence. It may have been brown. I don't remember. Our patient was in the bedroom, to the right of the front door. And she was the most enormous amount of human I'd ever seen in one place. Turns out, she wasn't that old, maybe in her thirties, probably younger than I am now. Turns out, the last time she'd been out of the house, six months prior, she'd weighed in at over six hundred pounds.

One only "weighs in" at some weight if it's important, like for a boxer or a wrestler or a patient like this. It was important because it was most of what'd killed her. And she was dead as fuck.

I got stuck in the front doorway for a second, caught first by the faces of her distressed family in the living room, secondly by the odor, something between fermentation and mildew and somewhere south of cheese. Lastly, I was caught by the sight of all that flesh. I understood why they'd called for extra hands.

The other crews, already on scene, were just rolling her off a dank full-sized mattress along the wall onto the floor, where the bottom of the trailer would give us a hard surface for CPR. Toward the head was my friend John, one of the best paramedics to ever polish a boot and one of my mentors. He would later die in the line of duty in a helicopter crash that would break my heart and those of a thousand others. But that night he wasn't dead. She was.

John tasked me with chest compressions and I immediately obeyed him. I stood on her left side, facing that dirty, little, urine-soaked bed and started that rhythmic pressing I've done hundreds of times since.

"Staying alive . . . staying alive . . . ha-ha-ha-ha . . . staying aliiiii—iiiiive . . . "

Turns out, that song is the perfect cadence, and perfect irony, for CPR. Even today, I sing it in my head when I'm doing compressions. That was the first time. On her. She was so big that instead of kneeling beside her like those neat and tidy American Heart Association videos, I was standing fully up, flexed at the waist, at the perfect height to pound on her chest. And pound I did. I may as well have stood on her for all the good I was doing.

Poor John, at her mouth with his laryngoscope blade, was in a deep squat, trying to get her intubated. I don't remember her face, which is not uncommon. It's a defense mechanism that happens naturally. And in the end, it doesn't matter. I didn't know her in her life, only in her death. But I remember John's face, running with sweat. In our tenure together, I would see him belly down in pools of vomit or splatters of gray matter, working at that same skill.

When I became a paramedic and it was me who was belly down, legs outstretched in the snow of New England or the broken glass of some desert highway or with the smoke of a fresh house fire in my nose while the whole scene watched me intubate the family dog, I'd think of John and try to do my best.

Chad, Mesilla 4-5, arrived soon after me, and to this day remembers the shock of watching me do chest compressions standing up. We worked her for a long time. And once we called her, we still had work to do. It was a long night, getting her out of the house and into the medical examiner's van. We used our rescue tools to cut the side off the trailer, strapped two backboards together, and slid her out. It took twelve people.

We went back to the firehouse to clean and restock, and we spent some time telling stories, decompressing. From there, in the small, still hours of the early morning, I went to my new boyfriend's house, seeking comfort. He did his best. Later he'd be my fiancé, then my husband, then my ex-husband, now a distant and rueful memory. He would become the patron saint of delicate stomachs, who couldn't bear the stories I needed to tell. His distaste for my tasks, and the way my job stress infected him by contact, would drive me to the pen. I learned to write as a way to cope.

It was then that I started to know that not everyone knows what I know. Not everyone has the will to see what I see. Not everyone has a job like that. It was then that I'd start to just barely feel the weight of that badge, that irrevocable rise to duty toward a bell that never stops tolling. That was the first time I knew it would be hard. And John hadn't even died yet.

Now, after two decades of watching people live and die, I still struggle to shoulder the burden of it all. Sometimes my shoulders slump under the weight of the badge, or the weight of my white coat. No matter how many tools I have in my belt for coping with loss, sometimes I feel like I can't access them. There have been moments in my life that I was close to taking my own life. And

I'm not sure it would have surprised anyone who knows me well, nor anyone who has seen the same kind of shit.

The Twitterverse likes to tell suicidal people that the day they attempt suicide will be the worst day of their lives. They hashtag "only one direction to go from here" platitudes. Facebookers post mountain memes, showing something steep but surmountable. And suicidal people buy into that image of a ski slope stretching up ahead, one chairlift, inexorably pulled toward the top, on a clearly marked path. If they can just ride it to the top, they'll be able to dismount and stand triumphant, Instagram-worthy for their fortitude. But that's all bullshit.

Sliding down the other side, suicidal people realize there are valleys beyond valleys and mountains beyond mountains. The loss of that illusory peak is re-devastating.

A more fitting and arduous metaphor would be a cross-country snowshoe. A hike in deep, powdery snow that, even with the shoe, comes up to your hip, each step laborious and grueling. You fall down. Falling down in snowshoes is a total pain in the ass, especially when you're wearing a forty-pound winter pack. You can't "just" stand up. There's nothing to push against. You can't just put your hands in the snow and push yourself up. The snow disappears under your hands and then you're shoulder-deep in the drifts.

You have to get your shoes underneath you and flat. You have to get your poles into something with some purchase. You rock back and forth and heave yourself upward, quads straining against the knees, triceps pulling with all they can muster.

One of three things will happen. First, you may fall back again, planting your ass even deeper into the snow, making the next attempt harder. Or, perhaps, you summon so much energy that you rise fully onto your shoes, but the weight of your pack, full of inertia, carries you too far forward and you pitch onto your belly and face. If you really overshoot, you wind up picking the shoes up off their base and planting them, toe-first into the snow.

And without your arms it's impossible to push your way back onto your heels, impossible to get your feet flat again.

Your only choice then, is to roll to one side and turtle onto your back, pointing the shoes upright like water skis. Then, essentially, you're in the same position from which you started, but facing the wrong way on the trail.

God forbid your partner tries to help you get up, because they are just as likely to fall next to you, and then you're both turtling and struggling and eternally snow angel-ing, until your fingers and toes and butt cheeks go numb. At times, you have to rest in the struggle, because you're sweating too much. And you know that sweat-soaked clothes kill people in winter.

So you lay back in the cradling flakes until you start to shiver, then go at it again. Rocking. Heaving. Grunting. Pulling. Pushing. At some point, since you haven't actually died yet, you get upright again and start breaking trail.

The blue, winter sky and the barren trees and the glinting snow pass the sides of your vision. Some of that view is utilitarian, some of it arrestingly beautiful, halting your steps for a moment. You trudge on, never really understanding whether you're ascending or descending, but knowing that you toil. Then, a misstep or a rock or a sideways slope and you're on your back again. But, by the time you've gone twenty or thirty miles in snowshoes, you kind of get it. You get that falling is part of it.

Falling is to be anticipated and prepared for but not dreaded, because it's unavoidable. After you've gotten upright forty or fifty or sixty times, you learn that you can get up. And even if you couldn't, spring would eventually come. The snow would eventually melt, and then you could just walk out. That's what recovering from suicide is like.

When you get to the end of the trail and the snow has melted, you head into town and get a hot meal and a cold beer. You wash in the restroom sink, drying your hair under the hand blower. You look at all these other people, safe in their coffee shops and warm in their houses and sedated on their couches and you think, "I survived things you guys will never, ever understand. I've known things you will never know, and here I am. I'm here to taste the wine and smell the coffee and feel the carrot cake and hear the wind chimes and see the fluttering leaves on the poplar trees. And none of you can take that ability from me."

The scariest of people I've ever known was me. The ugliest of places I've ever seen was inside my own head. The darkest sound I've ever heard was my own heart in my broken chest. It used to be that I feared the return of that gaping chasm, that plummet, that bottomless cave, but no longer. Because now I know that life is not a bungee jump. It's not a skydive. It's not a lazy inner tube float down some placid river. It's not rolling, waving wheat fields and fucking daisies. It's a thousand-mile snowshoe. It's flat, with knobs and saddles. It's cold, with breaths of warm sun and still wind. It's hard, with moments of respite and ease. It's easy, with moments of terror and panic. It just is. So just keep moving.

Green Light

A ferry ride off Seattle with a veteran who feels like I do
Seattle, Washington. Early Spring.

I head for Pike Place Market, where I love to walk among the flowers, endless rows of fresh flowers. I hear the vendors shout prices and patrons shout questions. The place is full of energy and vibrancy and pungent fish flying through the air.

The seafood pricing reports, in the chaos of Saturday, represent the culture and the commodities of the region, just as the cattle price per head in Montana and the oil price per barrel in North Dakota and the wine price per bottle in Mendocino County reflect what's important to those ranchers and roughnecks and vintners. The border wait-times in San Diego and the traffic reports in Chicago help to direct business. The snowfall reports at Sierra Blanca and Sunday River entice the skiers. And the "baby bump" contests in Rexburg, Idaho, get the Mormon ladies excited.

Today, my friend (an army veteran) and I take a ferry from the Seattle harbor to Bainbridge Island and back. We both have PTSD, he from his service, me from my work. We take boat rides like this just to get away and have a specific period of time in which we're not responsible for anyone or anything. There's a space, a hollow sacred space in time, when you can reply, "I'm on the ferry" or "I'm on the train" or whatever, and no one can demand anything from you. Nothing happening in your life is going to make the ferry go any faster, nor bring the ports of call any closer together. It's a beautiful time of freedom from responsibility for disaster response.

We sit outside in coats and hats and gloves, alone on a bench that would be packed with tourists on a warm summer day. It's late afternoon, heading toward twilight, when we set off. The stars prick out one by one as we go. We pass the shores of the island studded with houses. Those house lights look so warm and cozy to me from here, on the cold water. For some reason, the lights of my own house have never seemed quite so inviting from the inside as places like this seem from the outside.

We ride the gentle current in silence for a bit, wind streaking our cheeks and coaxing the water from our noses. One house here, another there, one across the bay, they have green lights on. At one house, it's a porch light. At another, an upstairs bedroom is lit up. Someone even has his boathouse dressed in green like it's a mariner's St. Patrick's Day.

"What's with the green lights?" I pose.

He turns his head to look at me. An eyebrow raises. "You don't know? You . . . of all people?"

"Thank you for today's dose of inadequacy, but no, I don't know what the green, 'me of all people,' lights mean. Are you going to tell me or just sit there with that look on your face like an asshole?" We're both grinning.

He pauses. I wait.

"There's a new ad campaign. It's on YouTube and Facebook and TV."

He's silent for a minute. "These commercials, they show these people in the community. They're supposed to be veterans who've come back home, and in their normal jobs they are 'more camouflaged than ever.'"

This man, like me and like many of my friends, has seen and done terrible things that he'd like to forget.

"So," he makes the air quotation mark with his hand, "to 'show them your support,' you're supposed to turn one of your lights green. 'We may not be able to see them, but at least they'll know we're here.'"

Seconds pass, and I know it's not the gentle heave and thrill of the bow that makes me want to vomit. It's the confectioner's sugar sweetness of the latest salutation that turns my stomach in a way that Puget Sound cannot.

"'Thanks for your service,'" he air quotes again, "is the same now as saying 'Dear Sir or Madame' at the beginning of some letter. You don't actually mean 'dear.' You've never met these jerks in your life, but it's something you're supposed to say."

He continues, "Kind of like, 'How are you?' No one really wants to know. It's just common courtesy to ask. And I guess it's better than being accosted and assaulted the way some guys were when they came back from Vietnam. Or forgotten when they came back from Somalia. But still, all that Support Our Troops bullshit isn't for the vets."

"Who's it for?" I ask.

"It's for themselves. It's for the people waving the flags or dangling the ribbons. It's a tool to make themselves feel better for not actually having volunteered to serve. For knowing nothing about the conflict they've sent their sons into. It makes them feel better about never having put themselves in harm's way. They can find a way to feel a kinship they've not actually earned.

"No one ever actually wants to help. No one ever actually wants to know. If they did, they'd be volunteering at a VA clinic, pushing dudes around in wheelchairs and playing dominos. They may want to hear gore stories and horror stories, but they don't want to know about 3 a.m. on the bathroom floor, when something triggered you while you were out with your friends and you had to excuse yourself so you could go shake for a while next to the toilet.

"You wanna know what you can do for me? Do my fucking laundry! Make me a fucking sandwich! Better yet, make a bunch of sandwiches and wrap them in foil and stack them in the freezer so that when I have to come home and throw up and shiver on the bathroom floor for a while, I can eventually get up and turn on the oven and put one of those tin foil sandwiches on the center rack and I can lie down on the kitchen floor with a fucking forty of Ballantine's and while I'm trying to dust the desert sand out of my eyelashes, that sandwich will get warm and when I can smell it, I can come back into the present and I can sit up and peer into the oven, all warm and orange-red, and grab that sandwich and put it in my mouth and feel warm for just a minute."

"That," he screams to the black liquid night, "that would make me feel appreciated!"

His voice softens to a whisper, as if his own echo from Puget Sound startled him. "Pay my cell phone bill so I can call my mom. Pay my electric bill so I can leave the lights on all night. Pay for me to see a shrink. That would probably help me, too. Though the sandwich is probably cheaper."

He takes a breath. "I don't need anything, really, from anybody. If I need it, I go out and work for it. But every now and then, a hot sandwich would be nice."

The ferry bumps softly into the pilings back on the Seattle side, signaling that our sacred time, free from the world, is over.

Exit Strategy

Musings from the road and the cold
Sioux Falls, South Dakota. Deep winter.

It's twenty-five degrees below zero without the windchill, and the snow is accumulating by the foot despite the thirty-mile-per-hour winds that try to drive those flakes across the plains. I limp into some local hotel, ready for a night inside.

Any time I check into a hotel, I'm prepared to leave it immediately, to evacuate it. That's because of 1991. The Gulf War had just started and the nation was jittery. Our flight to Dallas was the first I'd had in which security was visibly intensified. Those green night-vision videos of high velocity rounds scorching the far desert played in our head as we lay down for sleep on the eleventh floor of the Westin Hotel. I was only thirteen. I shared a room with my friend and two other dancers. We were a group of twenty or thirty and we'd come to town for a dance convention.

At 2 a.m. the fire alarm went off. I can still remember the woman's voice on the loudspeaker: "Attention, Attention." The alert was followed by instructions, then repeated in French and Spanish. Out our doors we went. My young friend and I clutched each other and ran barefoot down twenty-two flights of stairs, alongside a throng of people. We came out the stairwell door and clustered in the parking lot. I remember counting twenty-two emergency vehicles around the hotel. It was cold. But it wasn't South Dakota.

• • •

Tonight in Sioux Falls there have been windchill warnings. The sky is so crystal clear, the stars seem to be drops of ice flung there and frozen to the black velvet bowl around us. It's twenty degrees below zero outside and nearing minus twenty-five.

The alarm sounds at 2:08 a.m. with a horn that still reminds me of General Schwarzkopf and the air-raid sirens. A man's voice, in English only, states, "An emergency has been reported. Please move to the exit doors using the nearest stairwell. Do not use the elevators."

A flashing strobe in my room is the only light until I click on the bedside lamp. First, I move to the room door and put my hand against it. It's cool. I put my eye to the peephole. I see no smoke. No people. I take a moment to smell and listen. Nothing but the opening and closing of doors along the corridor.

I bend down and start grabbing the clothes, the socks, the shoes, hat, gloves, balaclava, and coat that I'd stashed near the door. I don them. All of them. I take a few steps back into the room to grab the room key, my phone, and the bag that holds my wallet, keys, and laptop. I head out into the corridor where other bewildered guests are walking around, standing at their open doors and looking at each other. Ignoring them, I move left, to the stairwell that I already know is closest, and I begin the trek down. This time, it's only eight flights.

Once I move into the stairwell, the people behind me start to do the same. We encounter other guests from other floors going down and, surprisingly, a few people coming up. To my quizzical look they say, "This leads outside, so we need our coats."

It takes every ounce of me not to say, "No shit! It's twenty-five below zero plus windchill at two in the morning and you didn't think it through more than that?"

Ever since that morning in Dallas, terrifying for a thirteen-year-old already on edge about a country at war, I've kept, at a minimum, a pair of shoes next to the door of my room. I usually have clothes laid out and outerwear close by if it's a cold time and place. I have everything I would absolutely need like my driver's license, debit card, passport, car keys, and phone in one bag, also at the door.

Tonight, I know that the biggest threat is getting stuck outside. I'm extra prepared. It's just the way I am. Once a firefighter, always a firefighter. And sometimes I'm a bit prescient. I knew when I checked in tonight that we might have to evacuate. Often, I get those feelings and nothing ever happens. But sometimes I'm right. So, tonight, I have super warm socks, warm boots, hat, gloves, balaclava, and my Arctic Expedition coat next to the door. And I put every single bit of it on. That only takes me about twenty seconds. I logically figure that if there is no immediate, visible threat, then I have time for that, and only that.

Moving down the stairwell, I am amazed at the level of disrobe in which some of the guests appear. Many are in pajama pants or nightgowns with bare legs. Many in socks or slippers. Hardly any with hats or gloves. Even if this is a false alarm, if these people accidentally get locked outside, this is quickly going to turn into a mass casualty event. And a bunch of able-bodied people are going to be helpless.

Since the heat in the building is cranked and I awoke with a splitting headache, in my mind, the possibility of carbon monoxide poisoning is very real. So when I get to the ground-level exit door, I open it for a moment to assess the outside situation. Nothing seems amiss, so I plunk down on the floor next to the door. I leave my coat on but unzip it. I take my gloves off, leave my hat on. Eventually, after about an hour huddled at the base of the stairwell with ten other people, we get the all-clear to go back to our rooms. Upon my return, I lay things out again, but this time, I put the room key in my jacket pocket. I stuff the gloves and hat in pockets too. I put my socks directly on top of my boots, and I put my bag right next to everything, closer than it was previously.

I know all that seems like overkill and people probably wonder if I actually do that every time I sleep in a hotel. But I do. That Gulf War experience changed me because it scared me. And my career in the fire service changed me because it scared me. September 11 scared me. I've been taught to anticipate and prepare for the worst, as a professional. I do so in civilian life, too.

I tell my friends to try and picture themselves awakened by that same alarm, but this time, no lights come on. You sit up in bed and the top of your head gets warm. You smell smoke. You hear screaming. Could you actually get out of the room and out the door of the hotel? Could you find your shoes and your coat? Could you find them in the dark? Could you find them as you were crawling on the floor? Could you find your way to the exit if you were blinded?

When you check in, find your closest exit and remember it in turns: "Left out the door, end of the hall, right turn into the stairs." Count the number of doors between you and the stairwell. Put your shoes by the door. If you're in a cold place, put your outerwear where you can get to it quickly and blindly. When you get on a plane, count the rows to the closest exit and the second-closest exit. When you sit in a restaurant or theater or sporting event, find the closest evacuation route and a backup plan, knowing that it might be through the kitchen. If you're in Tornado Alley, know the lowest interior room with no windows in every building you go into. And if you're in a public place, know how you would hide from an active shooter or to where you would run. And don't ever, ever feel like a fool for leaving a place because it felt wrong.

When the planes hit the World Trade Center, some of the people on the upper floors who made it out before the buildings collapsed made it out with absolutely no time to spare. And they went down 180 flights of stairs in the pitch-black and heat. Those who dawdled, died. Those who ran flat out, lived. Drill yourself the next time you're in a hotel and see how quickly you can be out the door. It may save your life.

Hot Water

Washing away the Bakken and the ghosts of my own work
Livingston, Montana. Late winter.

I'm thankful for Teddy Roosevelt. He, some long-forgotten day, went to Montana and thought it was beautiful. He also went to Idaho and Minnesota and the Adirondacks. And sometime before he was vice president, before he became president himself, he went west. He went west, and he saw beautiful things and the potential for them to be exploited. From his influence then, the National Park System was born.

Roosevelt, along with a cooperative Congress, preserved some of the most spectacular land that North America has to offer. He could see the writing on the wall. He could see the way in which our relentless westward push would one day swallow all that was beautiful and sacred on this land.

He catalogued the species he found. He sent one of each to a museum that eventually became the Museum of Natural History and one of each to his own estate. Everything he found—deer, moose, caribou, antelope, wolf, bison, coyote, wild horse, wild boar, bear, trout, big cats—all of it went into his logbooks and into his collection.

He and his crew found them, bagged them, and sent them to record. They also ate them, tanned them, and wore them.

They saw the mineralization beneath the plains and between the mountains that would one day drive men to drill for oil and dig for gold. He made Theodore Roosevelt National Park in North Dakota and Glacier National Park in Montana, and if he hadn't, today there would be drilling rigs from Chicago to Seattle, uninterrupted.

I remember all this as I wend my way away from the Bakken and toward the Rocky Mountains. If I push long enough tonight, I know I'll get to one of my absolute favorite places on the planet. It's the Chico Hot Springs Resort and Day Spa, south of Livingston, Montana, somewhere between Billings and Missoula. It's tucked back near the top of Yellowstone National Park and it's like stepping back in time. It's a wicked-old hotel, with little rooms of iron beds and shared bathrooms with claw-foot tubs. There are a couple of little pubs on the property, surrounding the hot springs pool. But the real gem is the four-star restaurant just off the lobby.

I don't let the giant old woodstove and the mounted elk fool me into thinking I'll only get steak and potatoes here. This is culinary excellence from soup to nuts, accompanied by a world-class wine list. What outshines the food and the ambiance and the wine is the top-notch, gracious service by everyone associated with the place. Service doesn't even feel like the right term, so seamless and invisible is their professionalism. It feels more like friendship and kinship than a place I pay to feed me.

I walk through the rustic lobby and back along the length of the old-fashioned dining room to the small room in the back where the heavy hand-carved bar top and my favorite bartender, Kelby, reside. Along the route, I run into Colin, the general manager. It's late. There's hardly anyone around, but they welcome me. Colin sits at the bar with me, hungry himself, and we let Kelby decide what we're eating. A half-dozen small plates make their way in a leisurely parade from the kitchen, where the chef uses the late hour and the leftover stock to play.

Kelby, with his handlebar mustache, starched white shirt, and black arm ribbon, looks like 1880, but gastronomizes like 2018. He's not a chef, but he's made it his concern to know everything about this food in case his guests want to know everything about this food. Eventually, we wear Colin down and he goes to bed. Everyone who works here lives on premises. There is no town close by.

The lights in the restaurant are dark. The inn sleeps. The moon glow lights up the snow outside, but we're warm in here. Cozy. Kelby pulls a small step stool from under the bar and places it next to a set of very high shelves, stage right of the bar. I follow him with my gaze, wondering what he's going for.

There's an old, dusty bottle of tawny port on the shelf. He brings it down, clears the eastern Montana dirt from the cap and uncorks it. While he hunts for a strainer, I spend a few moments with the cork to my nose, breathing in forty years of grapes and time. It takes him a full five minutes to decant it for us, straining the sedimented casks, his strainer looking like the Thanksgiving cranberry dish by the time he's through.

While we wait for the oxygen in the air to work its key-in-lock magic, pausing every couple of minutes for another sniff, we talk. We talk about life. We talk about people. We talk about the fragile and ridiculous nature of man. We talk about mountains and cold and wolves. And when the port is ready, we drink. Slowly. Silently.

Each sip down the glass is different than the last. Every couple of minutes, one of us, from our respective side of the bar, declares what we're tasting.

"Raisin," I say. He nods.

"Almond," he says. I nod. Minutes of swirling and sniffing and sipping.

Then, "Figs." Nods.

"Mmm, walnuts." Nods.

"Woah! White grape juice."

"Hmmm . . . oh yeah!"

Sip. Sniff. Cradle. Swirl. Get transported.

"Dirt, arid dirt." Nods.

Quiet smiles. Deep sighs. Eventually, the tiny glasses are empty, the bar is dark, and we're totally blissed out.

"Good night."

"See you next time."

I nod and rise, tiptoeing back through the darkened restaurant and into the lobby and up the old stairs, the ancient wood announcing every step. In my tiny single room, with the iron bed and the enamel washing pan in the corner, I strip off my clothes and put my pink and purple polka-dot bikini and flip-flops next to the door, for the morning.

Sometime very early I don them, both incongruous on this frigid Montana morning. I wrap a towel around myself and put my knit cap on my head. I walk down the long narrow hallway, turning a couple of ninety-degree corners, passing other single and double rooms with heavy wooden doors to match my own, skirting past the bathrooms of white tile and claw-foot cast iron, to the hidden staircase. It looks like a wall at the dead end of a corridor, but a solid shove and it opens to me.

I descend a steep set of stairs, rubberized and salted, and land in a dark corner of the pool deck. This is the hot pot, the half-Olympic-sized pool of volcanic water that draws folks from across the country. This is the Chico Hot Spring. And this is why I've come. To debrief.

Every night, they drain the enormous pool. And, every dark and early morning, the mountain fills it up again. There's a big white pipe that leads directly from the mountain's interior to this pool. And the water that comes out of it is so hot that one can only sit under it for a few moments, thereafter drifting naturally away to the places where the frozen bottom of the pool and the frigid winter air have tempered it some. At this hour, the pool is technically closed to the public, and at the ten-foot-deep end of it, there are only about three feet of water. By seven in the morning, when the pool opens again, it will be halfway full, not to reach its high-water mark for another ten hours.

In silence, I leave my sandals and cap and towel under cover of the awning and scurry on freezing feet across the searing cold pool deck, onto the pebbled surface of the shallow end, heading toward the cloud of steam at the deep end. As the pool wall ascends above my head and my skin burns with the icy air, my toes finally hit the warm water. I wade in swiftly, breaking the silence only with small, ecstatic gasps. Since the water, at its deepest, comes only to my waist, I sit. I'm just at the edge of the imperceptibly rising water, stretching my feet out in front of me.

I lay back and dunk my head, then simmer with my shoulders and chin below the warm dividing line. In less than a minute, the water in my hair freezes and my eyelashes reflect and refract the faintest of the dawn like they're studded with Swarovski crystals. All it takes is a little dunk under the water, and the ice melts again.

I float on my back for a while, letting the current from the mountain pipe guide me around the pool, and above me, a billion unfettered stars shimmer and fade toward morning. The new, clean water scrubs everything from me and the big, big sky absorbs my steamy breath, ferrying all the terrible things I've heard and said and seen in my career up into the vacuum of space and stars. A residue washes off me and falls to the bottom. Tears run from my eyes, freezing on my cheeks, and when I dip my head again, they salt the sulfurous water and fill the pool, again imperceptibly higher.

When I'm wrinkled like a prune, I make the mad dash, a Penguin Plunge in reverse, to my shoes and my towel and my warm room. I leave Chico, blissful and hopeful, warmer than I was the day before. That bit of hot mountain water is enough to sustain me for a little while, enough to make me believe in life and the world and humans.

Mineral Spirits

Ghosted towns of the West
Jerome, Arizona. Not summer.

If there's something I take from Jerome, Arizona, it's the same thing I take from each of these towns: ghosts. All of them—gold mines, copper mines, silver towns, coal mountains, fishing camps, logging woods—have the same sense of spirit. I don't mean spirituality. I mean spirit. I don't mean *joie de vivre*, I mean spirit. I don't mean religion or Holy Spirit. I mean ghosts.

In old brick watering holes with heavy, carved-oak bar fronts and copper bar tops and pressed-tin ceilings, there linger more patrons than there is the booze to serve them. In brothels and ill-repute houses, there floats, ethereally, something more than memory but less than substance. In stacked boarding houses, on the sides of a thousand carved out hills, sallow men in worn shoes roam hallways lined with doors that once represented their only respite from the unfailing and unchanging company they kept all day. These places, remote, inhospitable by the season, are full of hope and desperation and sweat and whiskey.

They echo with a music borne of labor and lust. They vibrate with the noise of crushed rock, locked forever in its angle of repose. The air is thick with the dust of detrital rust. The floors are full of dancing feet and sawdust. Ceilings are hung with tobacco smoke. Walls are painted in lamplight, flickering still.

Even I transform in these places. My dress lengthening, my skirts ruffling, my collar heightening, my sleeves reaching for my wrists, my boots narrowing on my feet, and me floating the way these ghost women around me do. I love to stand on an old porch, with its crooked boards and rough hew, gazing over the irregular horizon and watching the same sun cross the sky. I look for the evidence of old buildings, lost in flame or fallen into the brush, and I smell the stories in their foundations, amid the concrete lime and the mortar of bricks.

Those stories are universal in the West; only the color of the loot is different. They're the same in the north, only the temperature is different. Hardship and hard luck and hardscrabble. Heavy lifting and heavy hearts and heavy heads. The blisters of the pick and shovel. The cough of dusted lungs. Digging and drilling and blasting closer to the molten center of the earth and the promise of The Great Promise. Then abandoned.

Done. Gone. Evacuated and scavenged and left exhaustedly behind on the day it becomes, instead, The Great Lie. These are the places where no one really got rich like they thought they would. These towns are left to the wolves and the weather and the seasons, to lie there until the developers and the artists and the tourists come back. New people polish the copper bar and wander among the spirits. They are less worn, less forlorn, than those mineral ghosts.

While it's fun to visit some of these revitalized places, it's important to remember that they represent our garbage. They are scars left behind on what was once wild and pristine. And it's a cycle—boom-bust, build-abandon—that started with the earliest colonizers to hit the Atlantic coast and hasn't stopped yet. The Dutch in New Amsterdam, the French in St. Lawrence, the Portuguese in Newfoundland (*Terra Nova do Bacalhau*, "new found land of cod"), the English and their iron ore in Jamestown. They all started at the coast and moved inland chasing natural resources.

There is nothing wrong with taking advantage of the minerals and the timber and the food and the energy available within and upon the land. Where we get into trouble is in the displacement of established society and culture. The displacement of natural habitat. The short-sighted, poorly planned, ill-sustained use of something until it is either depleted or made worthless in a saturated market.

North America has a vast and diverse supply of resources that have both created and destroyed communities, families, and individual people. Now, more than ever, these communities have an opportunity to influence how those resources are harvested. But it's not simple. There is a difference between extraction and exploitation. Toeing that line requires close cooperation between the corporations behind the drilling, the digging, or the cutting, and the cities, counties, and states where the oil, the copper, and the trees grow.

Oil and gas development, mining operations, industrial fishing, and logging are not going away. They can't. The entire First World depends on them. Even the greenest and most socially altruistic of us use way more resources than we imagine, solely out of ignorance of manufacturing, shipping, and technology.

If we drive a vehicle, we are utilizing more than just oil and gas and the trucks, trains, pipelines, tanker ships, and refineries that process them. We are also using plastic, copper, iron, rare earths, molybdenum, questionably-sourced textiles, silica, and thousands of gallons of water. In using a telephone, whether it's a landline, a smartphone or a dumb phone, we are using oil, gas, coal, copper, gold, plastic, rare earths, platinum, and thousands of gallons of water.

In watching our favorite professional sports teams, we are not just responsible for the tickets and the team merchandise we buy. We are also responsible for their cross-country airplane rides and the airports and control towers that land them. We are responsible for the resources, land, and neighborhoods subsumed by their stadiums. The plastic, paper, and edible garbage that goes in the landfill after their games. The radioisotopes used in the X-ray machines and CT scanners that take pictures of their injuries. The water it takes to grow their fields, flush the toilets in their ballparks, and launder their uniforms.

In following them, we create the necessity of their headquarters and their internet marketing campaigns, as well as the electricity to run both. In observing their games, we require the power for radio antennas, newspaper presses, television receivers, and the rocket boosters that launch satellites into space so we can watch in real time.

Our work emails and our social media posts require enormous, redundant, temperature-controlled data centers that suck huge amounts of power and water from the grid to keep track of our vacation photos, our political rants, and our financial transactions.

This book was written on paper with a hundred plastic pens, then typed over the years onto a series of throw-away laptops, stored by Google's data centers, and then reprinted on more paper. It also required a couple of cars, a truck, fuel, flights, gear, food, communication, and all the mining, drilling, and agriculture that go into those things. After all, I didn't walk to all of these places. Our lives are too intertwined with the extractive industries to delude ourselves into thinking we can divorce ourselves from them entirely.

A better pursuit would be to pay attention to how much we consume, how closely it's produced to our homes, how much we waste, and how we allocate our personal time and energy. And if we happen to live in a community that has the blessing and the burden of a valuable resource, we should be actively engaged in how it's managed. That means showing up at city council meetings and voting in every local, regional, state, and national election. It means knowing the policymakers and getting an audience with them. Knowing the industry executives and getting an audience with them. Knowing our neighbors and defending those without a voice.

What would also help would be supporting those of us on the front lines of change. We could look at the men and women in uniform on the streets of our communities and provide them with what they need, including mental health care. We could insist that our towns be socially, fiscally, and infrastructurally sustainable. Insist that our civic leaders diversify our local economies when times are good so that there is something to fall back on when times are bad.

Most of all, we could spend less time on social media, typing against an injustice we barely understand a thousand miles away, when we could instead put boots to ground in our own towns, where we can actually effect change. If we did that, we'd leave behind fewer ghosts.

Desperada

Selling everything but my soul for gas and food
Somewhere in Ohio. Late spring.

It has been years since I set off from northern Maine on Thanksgiving Day. I haven't told anyone how broke I am. All the money's gone, all of it. My retirement savings. Everything I'd raised through my online campaign. Everything I'd begged and borrowed from my friends. Even the folded up hundred-dollar bills my mother had snuck into my backpack when I passed through my hometown. It's all gone. A couple days ago, somewhere in the South, I'd gotten as much as I could for my shotgun, the gun that kept me out of Canada and then kept me out of harm's way. Handing it over, I handed over a big chunk of physical security and an even bigger chunk of emotional security. Having to sell things off for cash, for food, for gas, this is a place I've been before. It's a place I swore I'd never come to again. Desperation. Hunger. Fear. Cold.

But here I am. And it is what it is. I lost any sense of pride or embarrassment regarding money years ago when the creditors were calling, and the landlords were threatening, and the guy came to haul away my car on a flatbed trailer. After a hundred collection calls, I just couldn't care anymore. That fact that I make poor fiscal decisions sometimes doesn't make me a bad person. It just makes me a bad investment.

Over the past few days, my shotgun money has taken me up into the Midwest. I'm headed to a job interview in Upstate New York, so I'm generally headed north and east. Somewhere, in some nondescript place of corn and freeways, I run out of gas. I coast into the parking lot of some truck stop back in the trees. It's a small place, not as rambling as those wide-open truck stops out west. But it's got a fair amount of traffic, both commercial and familial.

I drift into a spot at the end of the lot near the junction between the pumps for the tractor-trailers and the pumps for passenger cars. I make my way into the station store and charm a Magic Marker out of the kid behind the cash register with his terrible acne and his shy demeanor. Back at the truck, at Frankie, my rolling home, I pull the lid off my big blue Rubbermaid storage box. It's the one the holds the dresses and the panties and the high-heeled shoes that the Canadian border guards molested that Thanksgiving.

Using the Magic Marker, I write "TRUCK SALE" on the inside of the lid. I return the marker to the kid and walk back outside. I prop the lid up on the tailgate of my truck and start pulling stuff out to display it.

I turn Frankie into a little roadside stand. I only have a few things to sell that are worth anything at all to anyone, so I try to make it look interesting. I pull out the traffic flares, my orange triangles, a come-along hitch, a big tire jack, an array of bungee cords. I hang a trench coat and some dresses from Frankie's camper shell. There's some good rope. A portable gas can, empty now. A couple pairs of shoes, worn now. The fully mounted, studded winter spare tires are already gone. I begged someone to buy those a few counties back, even though studded tires were illegal there.

Once everything is arranged, I sit on the tailgate in the waning daylight. I hold the "TRUCK SALE" sign in my lap and put a toothy smile on my face. It's getting cold out. I make eye contact with each trucker as he rolls in, hoping one of them will stop with cash in hand. I flash the sign at folks coming out of the convenience store, carrying cans of soda, tins of dip, packs of cigarettes. Families in sedans cruise by, and I try to find the expressive balance between need and whimsy. If I look too desperate, people will think I'm just looking for money for booze or drugs. I need to make it clear that I'm just a nice girl who needs some fuel.

Occasionally I catch an eye, a second glance, a look of concern, and someone comes over to see what I'm doing. Mostly, it's truckers in their thirties or dads in their forties and fifties. "Are you selling the truck or the stuff in the truck?"

A couple of hunters buy some stuff, including the ammunition for a shotgun I no longer own. A Baptist preacher buys my "come-along." A man with his kids, and his wife urging him to keep driving, rolls down the window and hands me a twenty-dollar bill. A guy hauling a trailer of cattle buys my flares and pop-up triangles. A girl in a Prius buys a couple of dresses. A young hipster couple in a beat-up old Subaru stop to chat and fall in love with my story of road rambling and hardship. They give me some cash and half a bottle of cheap wine, with well-wishes and envy. I try to offer them some object or another, but they refuse to take it. The strict handouts make me uncomfortable, though my discomfort doesn't prevent me from taking them.

I see a young woman drive in, about my size, fairly well dressed but driving a shitty car. I pull out a special thing, a long, red, woolen trench coat from L.L. Bean that I envied for a couple of years in Maine before I bought it at the headquarters store in Freeport. It had seemed so important then, when I'd been dressing for dinner and had season tickets to the ballet. Now, in this parking lot in nowhere Middle America, it seems silly, superfluous. I walk it over to the fairly well-dressed girl in the shit car, and I tell her that I want her to have it. She thinks I'm crazy, but she takes it anyway. It helps me balance the universe.

After a few hours, I have enough money for a snack and a full tank, and I drive Frankie onward, toward my job interview. I've got to get there, since, clearly, I'm not going to be a paid author any time soon, and I'm hungry. I find a state park, essentially unoccupied and free of charge in this cold, early part of spring. When I pull into this man-made reservoir off the Mohawk River, I notice Frankie is sitting higher and driving lighter. I sleep in the back that night with so much less stuff around me, my most essential and meager of things only. I watch the fire for a while, waiting for tiredness. Then I go to bed hungry, catching an easy buzz off the wine the hipsters gave me. Tomorrow is an interview and hopefully a job.

I want to tell them that I'll have to live in this park until they pay me. I want to tell them that even if it's a shit job, I'm going to take it. But I won't. I'll do my best to look professional and comfortable. And, in the end, I'll get the job and do the work I've been avoiding, the work that isn't writing, that isn't traveling, but is nonetheless important. It'll turn out to be the same as all the others. And it will set me back on the road, soon enough.

The Punxsutawney's Phil

Four days, four groundhogs, and forty thousand visitors
Punxsutawney, Pennsylvania. Winter.

It's the home of the world's most famous groundhog, Punxsutawney Phil. "Punxsy," as the locals call it, hosts over forty thousand people once a year, in gloomy February. In the four days surrounding Groundhog Day, this sleepy hamlet of six thousand people bursts onto the national stage. Visitors come from all over the world to eat, drink, freeze, and hear the famous weather report.

All of these folks not only tax the local food and lodging establishments, but certainly the local emergency responders. I pull up to Central Fire Station and introduce myself. I learn that Punxsutawney Fire Department shares a small campus with the police department, public works, the tax assessor, the municipal court, and the library. A firefighter leads me into the library, which is the year-round home of Punxsutawney Phil. There are four groundhogs sleeping or milling about a glass enclosure in one corner of the building. On February 2, two groundhogs are taken up to Gobbler's Nob, and the most docile one is chosen to represent the town for the day. They don't seem to care much that I'm looking at them, unaware of their own celebrity.

The fire station next door is one of three companies that operate somewhat independently in that they choose their own equipment (some use Scott brand air packs, some use MSA brand, etc.), but they fall under the Borough of Punxsutawney, with a central budget and a central chief. They are an all-volunteer department with a fluctuating roster of nearly one hundred firefighters with about twenty people per company who contribute most consistently to the work of the department. It's about average for this size of town.

They are equipped with three pumpers, one tower/ladder, two heavy rescue/extrication trucks, one brush truck, and two water tankers. A general utility truck, a hazardous materials trailer, and a rescue boat round out the apparatus, adequate gear for the job. Most of the firefighters are hazmat trained at least to first-responder level and the department staffs a dive rescue team. The fire department is not the primary agency responsible for emergency medical response in the borough, but many are cross-trained at least to EMT-First Responder and all are CPR and basic first aid certified.

Medical response is provided by Jefferson County Emergency Medical Services, which has one full-time base at the local hospital with two staffed medic units and a spare that can be staffed by volunteers if the call volume demands it. The ambulance is staffed with a paramedic and an EMT-Basic, and the majority of their patients go to Punxsutawney Area Hospital, a forty-nine-bed facility that offers primary care, emergency care, and some limited specialty services. All critically ill patients are taken to Pittsburgh area hospitals, which is about ninety minutes away by ground in good weather. For patients needing more expeditious transport, helicopter ambulance service is provided by STAT MedEvac.

On a normal, non-Groundhog Day the local police department—which has one officer on duty per shift, on somewhat overlapping shifts—may run five to ten calls depending upon the time of year. That's pretty slow. In the two to four days surrounding February 2, the local police department draws on law enforcement officers from around the state to help provide a deterring presence, direct traffic, and handle the small disturbances that always come with having a large group of people congregated, especially when alcohol is involved. Officers come from neighboring boroughs, the state police, the sheriff's department, the probation unit, and liquor control enforcement. The National Guard also steps in to assist with traffic and crowd control. Alcohol is prohibited at Gobbler's Nob, the viewing platform just outside town, where the actual event is held. But plenty of visitors still imbibe around town.

Punxsutawney itself is a charming small town with a central square and lovely old homes situated in what is a pastoral and agricultural part of Pennsylvania. Just outside town, I find a mix of traditional rural homes, moderate-acreage farm establishments, and Amish farms free of electricity and modern mechanization. No sooner do I spot the yellow and black "buggy crossing" signs than I come upon one, decked out with orange triangle reflectors and taillights as required.

I ask the emergency responders a pointed question that had occurred to me as I careened around a horse and buggy I'd encountered on a curve. "Do the Amish access emergency response services and, if so, how do they do it?" The Amish community does, in fact, on occasion activate 911. And they fully expect and support the response of mechanized fire trucks and ambulances to put out house and barn fires—a real risk in old homes using gas lanterns—and to transport ill and injured members of the community. Their daily work is fraught, as it always was, with opportunity for injury, from being kicked by a horse to falling off the hayloft to the newer threat of gruesome car vs buggy accidents. In those, the car always wins. It's pure physics.

Though the Amish don't own cars and don't drive, many will pay members of the community to drive them to town to buy groceries or go to doctor's appointments. There's a sort of cottage industry in Pennsylvania for those who drive them to make extra money. Often a household will have a cell phone that they keep charged, but off, for use strictly in emergencies. For those that don't, there are payphones scattered throughout the community on which they can call the police or fire department. Often, per the local officers, they don't involve the police department in disputes unless it involves an "English" (non-Amish) person. Disputes within community members are handled internally.

All in all, with the limited resources they have, the public safety providers of Punxsutawney, Pennsylvania, keep visitors, residents, and groundhogs safe and healthy. And their little town is a great example of our need, as a society, for entertainment and distraction. Especially in cold February.

The Pagoda

The Indy 500 and a pop-up trauma center in the infield
Indianapolis, Indiana. Autumn.

I push back into the seat and snug my five-point harness, cup the headphones around my ears, and answer, "Ready," when the pilot asks. The acrid, almost sweet smell of aviation fuel is in my nose. The pilot pulls pitch and that roller coaster drop happens in my belly. Once we reach maximum ground effect, he eases the nose of the Eurocopter EC145 down and we gain forward momentum.

The Indianapolis Motor Speedway is the home of the Indy 500, the Brickyard 400, and motorcycle racing's Grand Prix. As we approach the track, empty today except for some construction workers driving heavy equipment, my host describes for me the boundaries of the actual event, of the actual crowd, which far exceeds the acreage of the track itself.

As a responder, I'm automatically anxious at the thought of more than three hundred thousand people all mashed together under the hot May sun, inhibitions lowered by copious amounts of alcohol.

It's almost silent here today. Certainly, it's much quieter now than it would be on race day. To me, it's quite eerie to be here when the track is deserted, but the rescue crews come here frequently when there are no spectators present, to pre-plan and to be available as drivers are running time trials in preparation for race day.

The director of Indiana University Health's LifeLine air medical service patiently waits for me to snap a few selfies with "Turn 1" in the background and then we make our way into the infield clinic. This little building is nondescript and resembles any number of tiny outpost clinics scattered across rural parts of the United States. But on race day this place essentially becomes a Level I trauma center, capable of handling the most serious medical patients.

Inside this cinderblock rectangle, a few offices are scattered around the edges, adorned with antique photos of the track and snapshots of drivers. Also tucked into the corners are storage rooms for EMS equipment, fire resistant overalls, a portable hazmat shower, and about a dozen automated external defibrillators, stored here for the off season.

The long, open center of the building, loosely partitioned into three sections, is where the action, the off-track action anyway, happens. Closest to the public entrance is the largest of the treatment rooms with eight gurneys lined up against the wall, separated by hanging curtains. At the head of each bed are cabinets with linens and bedpans and such. Beside each bed is a portable blood pressure/heart rate/oxygen saturation monitor. This is where the majority of the 150 to 200 patients who are seen in the infield clinic each race day are treated and released. That's notwithstanding the other 800 to 900 people treated for minor injuries at one of the fifteen first aid stations positioned around the track. Those who require treatment in the infield clinic are brought here by modified golf cart. Fans pay a lot of money to enjoy the race and the providers here always want them to be able to return to their seats if possible.

Inside the clinic, further down the center rectangle, is another, smaller room with five of those same gurneys, which are equipped for more critical patients. Each has a 12-lead cardiac monitor at the head, as well as portable oxygen and IV equipment. Against the opposite wall, about six feet away, are cabinets and bins of advanced airway supplies, chest tubes, central line equipment, burn dressings, and obstetrical kits.

The majority of injuries treated at the track over the last 113 years of service include minor ankle injuries and lacerations, sunburns and heat-related illness, dehydration and gastrointestinal distress, and lots and lots of alcohol intoxication. A few traumatic injuries from fights, usually as a result of that intoxication, bring in black eyes and broken teeth. However, every year, there are spectators who become more critically ill, in equal proportion to any city of three hundred thousand, who just happen to be at the race when their event occurs. These chief complaints include chest pain and myocardial infarction, stroke, diabetic emergencies, and epileptic seizures. Asthma attacks and bee-sting anaphylaxis round out the list of three to five people who have to be intubated and mechanically ventilated every year.

There is a portable pharmacy machine, as well as X-ray and basic lab capabilities on-site, though any spectator who requires either of those, or any higher level of care, gets transported to Methodist Hospital, an Indiana University Health facility and Level I trauma center that is a straight shot four miles down the road. For patients who are stable enough to be transported by ground ambulance, a private agency provides twenty to twenty-five ambulances inside the track, staffed with one paramedic and one EMT-Basic apiece. Transport is facilitated by an on-site dispatcher inside the clinic, who also communicates with the first aid stations and the "Pagoda," the hub of communication for the track.

The LifeLine helicopter is used for transport, specifically during the high traffic periods when fans exiting the raceway grounds can clog the surrounding roadways for three to four hours after the last drivers have crossed the finish line.

The spectator portion of the clinic is staffed by four attending physicians and four to six resident doctors from Methodist Hospital, as well as twelve registered nurses. On the roster there is also a law enforcement officer, several security staff, a LifeLine dispatcher, and attorneys for the track who interview everyone treated at the facility if they are awake and able to respond. On the walls are gridded maps of the track with color-coded and numbered locations of restrooms, concession stands, gift shops, entrance/exit gates, elevators, and parking and camping areas.

The fans outside the track—many of whom camp for days—are managed by, secured by, attended and transported by a conglomeration of local and state law enforcement agencies including City of Indianapolis Police, Indiana State Police, the sheriff's department, and a private security company, in addition to Indianapolis Fire Department and the private ambulance service. These agencies share a temporary emergency operations center just off the track, complete with its own helipad. Along with a mirror image of injuries and illnesses treated inside the track, the off-track campground also includes the risk of carbon monoxide poisoning from inappropriately parked RVs, burns from BBQs and illegal campfires, motor vehicle accidents, and violent incidents including fights and stabbings.

Back inside the clinic, the remainder of the space is dedicated to treating the drivers. There is a private treatment room that looks essentially identical to the spectator area, but it is staffed with its own crew of four or five physicians, a physical therapist, a trauma surgeon, and a neurosurgeon. There is also the added availability of X-ray, laboratory studies, cardiac monitoring, and ultrasound. The drivers' area is equipped with its own portable pharmacy for dispensing medications.

Any driver who strikes the wall is required to come into the clinic for evaluation. However, with race car, helmet, and suit technology these days, even the most hideous looking wrecks usually result in drivers walking away from the crumpled mess of their cars and over to the responding safety crew. The extrication crew is staffed with a physician trained in extrication and outfitted in the same orange, fire resistant jumpsuit. Often, even drivers who require extrication can still, once cut free, walk to the waiting chase ambulance, go to the clinic, and be released. There are somewhere between two and ten drivers treated in the clinic every race day.

Though rare, a critical or fatal injury to a driver makes quite an impact on the clinical staff at the track. They get to know the drivers over time, not only by seeing them at every race around the world (many of the physicians travel internationally with the International Council of Motorsports Sciences), but also through annual physicals, complete with an optometrist's dilated-eye exam, and fit-for-racing follow-up evaluations, which are required for any driver who has previously suffered a concussion or needed hospital admission. They get to know the racers' families, and, as auto racing is often handed down from one generation to the next, these physicians may watch drivers grow up from infants. Many of the physicians get started at the raceway while they're still resident physicians, and they love it so much they stay on for the duration of their careers. They watch the older drivers play pranks on the new guys, and they check and re-check their OB kits when the racers' wives are expecting.

The commitment of the clinical staff goes beyond race day itself. Any time drivers are running time trials there are a couple of physicians, a handful of nurses, and a ground ambulance on-site. Indiana University Health's LifeLine helicopter is also usually on-site.

One of the most sophisticated flight medicine agencies in the country, LifeLine has five Eurocopter EC145s, one BK 117, and three ground mobile intensive-care units. Crews are able to warm blood and chill breast milk, both of which they carry. For babies, they are able to transport neonatal Isolettes. And for patients in shock or cardiac arrest, they can manage intra-aortic balloon pumps, ventricular assist devices, and occasionally extracorporeal membrane oxygenation (ECMO) machines supported with onboard liquid oxygen.

Their protocols include induced hypothermia for cardiac arrest, high-frequency ventilation for pediatric patients, rapid sequence induction for intubation, a sepsis protocol with early antibiotic administration, and ultrasound guided procedures. The adult/pediatric team includes a clinical staff of one registered nurse and one paramedic, and the neonatal/pediatric crew consists of a registered nurse and a respiratory therapist. All clinical staff members are not only cross-trained to match their partner's certification, but also trained as aviation communications specialists, staffing the LifeLine communications center at Methodist Hospital in two-person shifts as part of their regular work.

In case of poor visibility, the aircraft and pilots are instrument flight rated (IFR), and the program has ten IFR beacons around the county, including at all the regional airports, the downtown heliport, and every Indiana University Health system facility. Most air medical transport companies are not instrument flight rated. They utilize a state-of-the-art computer-aided dispatch and flight-following system and even have the capability of direct communication with field units through the Metro Aviation smartphone app, including text-message updates and GPS coordination.

LifeLine, as part of the racetrack medical staff, works closely with the area hospitals including the VA Hospital, Wishard Hospital (which has a dedicated burn unit), Riley Pediatric Hospital and Trauma Center, and, primarily, Methodist Hospital, which is part of the IU Health program and a short, three-minute flight from the speedway. Methodist Hospital is a Level I trauma center, a designation indicating the most advanced capabilities, with a large, sixty-bed emergency department, including four dedicated trauma bays. More than 120,000 emergency patients seek care in that ED per year.

Through the coordinated effort of motor-sports-trained physicians, specialized nursing staff, ground and air emergency medical services, law enforcement, racing safety crews, fire department, and communications specialists, the spectators and crew are able to return to the Indianapolis Motor Speedway healthy and eager, year after year.

Bitches Be Cray

Why there aren't more women in this book
Portland, Maine. Deep in the Edit. Almost spring.

There is a paucity of feminine voices in this book. That's neither oversight nor narcissism. It's a function of both the paucity of women in the professions I've profiled here, and in the closed, defensive, possessive posture we often take. I've had some wonderful girlfriends in my life, but the majority of my friends are men. It's only natural. I've spent the majority of my adult life working with them.

Women can be difficult for other women to work with, especially in any industry where they represent a minority of the roster. It is one of the great puzzles of my life, and an important problem for which I don't have a solution other than to hire more women. Women have been present as firefighters for centuries, since before Benjamin Franklin. But along with Franklin's professionalization, formalization, and commodification of fire protection in America, came the institutional exclusion of women in the paid services.

Firefighting jobs on full-time, fully paid departments are extremely competitive, especially during times of economic downturn. That's because they're good jobs. And for a couple of centuries, those jobs were deemed appropriate only for the coarser gender. But that hasn't kept the strongest, most pragmatic, "no bullshit" women of the United States from rising to fill the empty bunker boots that line the walls of volunteer firehouses.

Since the late seventies, most major metropolitan areas have employed women firefighters, but often as 1 or 2 percent of the total staff. Now, in the twenty-first century, that percentage has increased, but it is still nowhere near a quorum. Change is slow in the fire service. It's like turning an aircraft carrier . . . using oars instead of engines. It's a shame. Because some of the baddest motherfuckers I've ever worked with in the fire department have been women.

The nature of being an extreme minority within an already niche population is that one person immediately comes to represent the whole of their demographic. One Black man in a caucus is expected to speak for all Black men. One Asian man in a boardroom is presumed to represent all Asians, a vast and diverse proportion of humanity. One woman in a blue shirt on a fire truck suddenly represents all women who've ever worn a uniform of any stripe. And that's a problem.

It's problematic because we often don't like each other. It's a real thing. Women in the fire service, especially in mid-sized, "professional" career departments, hate each other. It must be something to do with needing to prove yourself, to prove the capabilities of all women everywhere, all the time. We must not trust the other women to do the job as well as we do. We must feel threatened.

I've seen women in these ultra-competitive environments purposefully cut each other down, undermine, sow chaos, stoke the fires of suspicion and rumor. Logically, we, as women, should never do that to each other. When one of us fails, we all fail. But these behaviors aren't rooted in logic. They're rooted in fear. There's the constant fear of not measuring up. There is fear that our missteps, natural along any professional learning curve, will be characterized as un-fitness for duty. Those fears are rooted in past experience for most women.

A man who gets injured on the job, who requires physical therapy and a temporary light-duty assignment, is respected as someone who worked hard and gave their all in a dangerous profession. When a woman gets hurt on the job, there's an immediate refrain of, "See, this is why women shouldn't be firefighters."

In my own experience, in a single department, I saw men who died of prostate cancer, lung cancer, and alcoholic asphyxiation get buried with full honors. But watched a woman who had to have a hysterectomy for cervical cancer be told that she needed to take hormone replacement therapy so she'd be easier to deal with (even though her ovaries had been preserved and she wasn't in surgical menopause).

In recounting my trip around the country, in which I dove as deeply as time allowed into each community, I hoped that my voice would suffice as the feminine perspective. But it doesn't. I don't represent every woman in uniform, despite the experiences that are common to our lives. There are undoubtedly women in emergency services who will find things to disagree with in these pages. But their voices aren't a part of this book, for two reasons.

First, there weren't that many women doing the work in the places I profiled. And if there were, they weren't commonly in leadership roles. In the paramilitaristic structure of the fire service, and even more so in law enforcement, it is "the brass" who fill the role of public information officer. It's the lieutenants and captains and chiefs who answer my questions. For a lower rank personnel to speak to me off-the-cuff, as a representative of their agency, would be an egregious breach of protocol approaching insubordination. A fireable offence. And if the rank and file of the nation's protective services have a deficit of women (and people of color) within the station house, then the admin building is positively barren of them.

The lack of women in leadership roles in these agencies is a persistent problem, persisting around North America two decades into the twenty-first century. Then, there's the other thing. Women won't talk to me.

It's that same old thing. Women bristle at another woman coming into their space, getting close to their men. Additionally, they often detest being singled out or featured, because they are punished for being singled out and featured. One of my early instructors, a woman, was one of a pair of the first women to be hired in what is now a well-known, often-studied, huge, successful, progressive fire department. She spoke to our class about how difficult it was to have reporters from the local metro news media following their time in the academy. The academy is hard, everywhere, for every recruit. It's physically, intellectually, and emotionally difficult for every single firefighter or police officer who goes through it.

The academy, like the rest of the job, is a fishbowl of scrutiny and a litany of tests, both in formal evaluation and in social assimilation. The last thing any rookie wants is more attention or additional benchmarks. But that's what the first minorities often get. So, as they grow into their careers, they wise up. And when they see me coming with my pad and pen, they run the other way. And I don't blame them. Because I know that sometimes bitches be cray.

Gravediggers

The housing boom and bust of the early millennium
Buckeye, Arizona. Spring.

"No one lays off firefighters."

That's what we all thought before 2008. No firefighter thinks that anymore.

Buckeye, Arizona, is nearly four hundred square miles of sand and scrub. It's ringed by modest desert hills and neighbored to the east by the multi-municipal Phoenix megalopolis. Buckeye is the westernmost incorporated suburb of Phoenix, giving it the advantage and the burden of almost limitless growth potential. It was precisely that open space that turned Buckeye into the epicenter of the early millennium's housing explosion.

Buckeye had a modest population of 6,537 at the 2000 census that mushroomed, at a wildfire pace, to over 50,000 people by 2010, a 678 percent increase, and climbing. Fire Chief Bob Costello came to the city from the state fire marshal's office in 2004 and was promoted to chief in 2007, near the top of a long, precipitous, and catastrophic slide in the housing market that hit the Phoenix metro area, and Buckeye in particular, harder than most of the country.

Costello says that Buckeye's exponential growth and subsequent retraction was "like nothing [he's] ever seen." He, a man of the fire service since the late 1970s, used that phrase over and over throughout our conversation in describing the community, the artificiality of market prices, the pattern of growth, and the loss of the revenue that accompanied the exodus of taxpaying homeowners. He also used it to proudly describe the unity and strength of character with which his firefighters have come through the process.

Most cities, as they expand, do so in a somewhat concentric pattern from the center of town, dependent upon topography and property rights. Buckeye grew "like a dalmatian," says Costello. It grew in widely separated "spots" of master-planned communities and clusters of tract homes, all in various shades of beige. Normally a town of 55,000–60,000 people, as Buckeye is now, should have roughly three fire stations to provide the level of fire protection and life support that communities in America have come to expect. Buckeye Fire Department has six stations, with plans for a seventh that were mothballed just prior to breaking ground.

New home construction was so feverish in the mid-2000s that people would camp for days in line outside home builders' trailers. The demo trailers sat in neighborhoods that didn't even have model homes standing yet. Lottery systems and early buy-in fees were the norm for developers in the region, and it was not uncommon to have fifty thousand dollars in equity growth in the five months it took to construct a home.

The rapidity of construction presented numerous logistical challenges for emergency responders, especially in the lag time of accurate mapping behind road creation. Costello says, "There were times that on one end of the street people were moving in, and literally on the other end of the street, the road infrastructure was just being cut." And that was happening all over the valley— not just in Buckeye—which added to the burden already upon the valley-wide automatic aid system dispatched by Phoenix Fire Department's nationally recognized dispatch center.

The satellite nature of these master-planned communities made providing a high level of service very costly. From his office in the historic portion of Buckeye, some of those developments are forty-five minutes away. For a metro area that is accustomed to four-minute response times, that's unheard of.

Each one of Buckeye's fire stations, once the lights are on, costs approximately $1.4 million per year in operating costs, in line with national averages. That cost goes on forever. Once it's built, it's very difficult to turn the lights back off again. Citizens will generally not accept a closure.

During the upswing, the city was growing so quickly, building new stations and taking delivery of shiny new trucks, that the labor pool of qualified firefighter applicants actually became somewhat shallow, due both to the sheer number of bodies needed to fill seats on the rigs and because every other fire department in the state was also hiring. The Phoenix area was cranking out training academies like a pasta maker.

Those circumstances gave Buckeye a relatively young, inexperienced corps of firefighters. "We doubled the size of the department in eighteen months." But necessity is the mother of invention. Thus, Buckeye Fire started a very aggressive, intensive training program that continues today. "We basically tried to replace experience with really good training," says Costello. There was no other way.

It was scary for everybody. The city's senior management was happy to have growth, but afraid of not being able to keep up with it. For the newly promoted captains, many of whom had only three years of experience, there was the anxiety of wondering whether they would end up in a situation they weren't prepared for. The sense was that growth was so fast that one day a person was brand new and the next day he was seasoned.

Because the department changed so dramatically in such a short period of time, it never got to develop an organizational culture. Chief Costello says, "We missed out on some of the traditions of the fire service, and that's both good and bad." Buckeye Fire Department has a unique culture that may be the reason the department has survived and become stronger, leaner, closer, and more appreciative than it would otherwise have been.

From the peak of hysteria in the American housing market and a time of comfort and plenty in public safety, post-9/11 the tide began to turn and Buckeye's newest residents, tied up in adjustable rate mortgages and houses that cost three hundred dollars a month to air condition, felt the first waves of recession. Then the tsunami of the subprime mortgage crisis hit them square in the mouth. Equity values plummeted as entire streets were foreclosed at the same time.

Because the fiscally smart thing to do became foreclosure, many homeowners simply packed their belongings, stuck their keys in an envelope, and mailed them back to the bank on their way out of the subdivision. As for the folks who remained in their homes throughout that process, most were no longer paying their property taxes, the main source of revenue to pay off six fire stations, six pumpers, two ladder trucks, two brush trucks, a technical rescue outfit, two command officer SUVs, a fleet of staff vehicles, salaries, and benefits. The equipment was more than adequate to do the job, but it was also expensive.

Overnight, everything was on the chopping block. "Not a day went by when layoff contingency plans weren't requested by the city manager," says the chief. All of a sudden, the very real possibility of laying off firefighters was upon Chief Costello and his labor union counterparts. "The very next budget cut had actual names attached to it," he says.

The department and the city itself took extreme measures to prevent layoffs. They survived by the skin of their teeth without having to send anyone home without a paycheck. That means they gave up pay raises and holiday pay, took on more responsibilities, lost benefits, lost uniform allowances, had zero dollars to replace equipment, didn't promote, didn't hire, ran short-staffed, had zero overtime, prayed staff wouldn't get hurt and trucks wouldn't stop running, and enlisted the community to advocate to policymakers to preserve some level of service commitment. Rumors of imminent layoffs in Buckeye made their way across the region by bush telegraph. I heard firefighters in neighboring departments say, "Guys in Buckeye are hauling trash and digging graves in the cemetery, bro."

The fire chief and the police chief tried to figure out a way to manage and lead and maintain a trace of morale, all while debating layoff procedures. "It was one of the tougher times in my whole career. Here you're looking at all these young faces, young families," says Costello.

Even Buckeye Fire's own staff got sucked into the housing crisis with everyone else, overextending themselves into loans that were based on virtually unlimited overtime and rock-bottom interest rates. They were unaware that the overtime would become absolutely nonexistent and the interest rates would start climbing one percentage point every six months, with no maximum. Like everyone else, many firefighters were foreclosed on and faced imminent unemployment. They were fairly new on the job, with a short resume to present anywhere else.

They were also still running calls, lots of calls. The same calls everyone else across the valley was running. When people call 911, they don't care what the city's bottom line is. When someone's having chest pain, they are unaware that their first due truck is out and that because they chose to live at the fringe of the metropolis, their second due truck is fifteen critical minutes away. When someone's trapped in a crushed motor vehicle, they are incapable of knowing that the ladder truck coming to extricate them is one crew member short, making the task that much harder.

While there was a brief dip in response volume as homes started to clear, it immediately rebounded as Buckeye Fire Department became the social services agency and primary care provider for sixty thousand people who were, themselves, in distress. Domestic violence incidents went through the roof, while, surprisingly, the number of house fires did not. As opposed to individualized financial events in which people sometimes burn their homes for the insurance money, these run-of-the-mill American workers found themselves in the same boat as everyone else and simply turned over the keys. And public safety in the town of Buckeye grabbed on with both hands and rode the wave, all the way to the trough, which Chief Costello hopes is past.

The department and the City of Buckeye committed to avoiding layoffs at all cost, something Costello is not 100 percent sure he would do again, given the chance and given hindsight. It was hard to avoid. Everyone picked up extra duties as positions went unfilled. When it came time to negotiate with the city, the fire department was asked to pick up some additional municipal work in order to preserve jobs. And that work has become legendary among firefighters in the greater metro area, accurate or not.

Chief Costello clears up the rumor mill for me, but he admits that Buckeye Fire Department has taken on some landscaping, maintenance, and funeral service duties for the small municipal cemetery owned by the city. They augment the sole caretaker there. Members of the community have expressed to Costello that they don't like to see their firefighters having to do that kind of work, but also can't think of a better group of people to support them in their times of grief with the loss of a loved one and their interment at the cemetery. For many of the firefighters, it was rewarding work that helped ease the survivor's guilt they felt after not being laid off when so many city employees had been.

The fire chief's biggest fears during the recession were twofold: being able to provide an appropriate level of service and keeping his crews safe. How do we keep boots on the street in the face of strict budget cuts? Today, his biggest fear is repeating the whole event. The housing market, along with the economy in general, has begun to rebound, but at a very unpredictable rate. "History tends to repeat itself," Costello confides.

So, though the department is much stronger and leaner, takes better care of its equipment, and has redesigned the way it does business, there is still the worry that things beyond local control will again tip the scales. For the first time since before the housing bubble burst, the department has been approved for one new captain-level, forty-hour-per-week position that allows for the promotion of a new captain, a new engineer, and the hiring of a new firefighter. That will be the first upward movement in some time.

Somehow, Buckeye Fire Department survived the downturn without having any firefighters simply walk away. The standard support systems were in place through the employee assistance program, the city's public safety chaplain, and health insurance benefits. But there was also a culture of true camaraderie, support, and nearly willful defiance of the adversity that just kept coming. "In the fire department, you just don't quit. You decide you're going to weather it," Costello says with conviction.

As for himself, Costello's been on the job long enough to retire, and while he's working on his exit strategy, he's in no hurry. "Frankly, there were days [during the recession] that I hated coming to work. I just had a sick feeling in my stomach. It was like an ongoing, long-term, bad dream."

At every yearly physical, he could see the tangible effects the stress was having on his body, readily apparent in his bloodwork. He and his battalion chiefs regularly sat down, in person, with their crews and their union representatives and weathered the storm and its resultant emotions together. Having been in the fire service so long, Costello has a network of peers to whom he can vent, and he realized during that time that he and his department were not alone: "You saw that they were miserable too."

As things continue on a careful upswing, wages have been restored, trucks are consistently fully staffed, some benefits have been restored, holiday pay is back, plans are in place for reasonable equipment replacement, and Costello and his wife are working together to figure out the best time for both of them to exit.

"You have to manage yourself through retirement," he says. He doesn't want to be one of those firefighters who are miserable once they're off the job. And, most importantly, he wants to have a succession plan in place that allows him to hand over the keys to the chief's office to someone fully trained, experienced, and qualified to handle the job.

When asked for words of advice to offer other public safety agencies around the country, booming or busting, Costello encourages open communication, a strong relationship with labor leaders, and a partnership with law enforcement and emergency medical providers in the community. "The police chief and I sat down in the very beginning and agreed not to battle each other," he says.

"Management and labor have to be able to sit in the same room and talk. Neither is going to like the outcome, but there must be a mutual understanding all the way through," Costello explains. In Buckeye's case, each player had different views of a layoff plan, none of them great. The union wanted layoffs to be based on seniority, which puts young firefighters with young families and short resumes out on the street. The city manager wanted preservation of paramedic employees, who are also the most expensive and have the highest liability insurance costs. Other departments have encouraged early retirement, which is quite cost-effective, but results in a loss of institutional memory and valuable experience in an industry where the stakes are so high, often life or death.

Chief Costello encourages struggling cities to remember their community members, who are also voting constituents of local policymakers. "You can't be afraid to explain the outcomes and consequences that come directly out of policy decisions." And Costello encourages those cities that are booming, or at the dawn of a boom, to think about managing growth with a solid fallback plan in place. When it comes to keeping up with growth in infrastructure, he suggests chasing it a bit instead of trying to stay ahead of it, which represents a radical paradigm shift for the fire service.

The chief suggests pre-planning for fiscal events in the same way we pre-plan for major incidents. And again, forces beyond local control, or even national control, will continue to influence fire service delivery in the United States, especially for departments that are the primary EMS provider for the community.

He describes his city's recent history of unfettered boom and subsequent near-collapse as a wake-up call for the fire service, regionally and nationally, saying, "hopefully we've learned from it."

I once lived in the same metro area that Chief Costello had a part in protecting. And I worked in the same industry, wore the same uniform, swore the same oath, just to a different department. I left there just before the housing crisis.

Twice in my life, my boom or bust has coincided with the wider prosperity or austerity of the country. In 2008, for example, I was the poorest and most isolated I've ever been. I was in a time of transition, back in school, sitting in a classroom full time for the first time in thirteen years. I was out of uniform for the first time in thirteen years.

I'd decided to leave the emergency response world and go indoors. I was headed to PA (physician assistant) school but needed some science courses updated. So, for the first time in a while, I was a student, with no income. And I was utterly alone.

The nation was descending into the Great Recession and I was worried for myself and for our country. I started learning. I learned what I needed to live, and what I could live without. I learned that people will buy almost anything on Craigslist, and I sold it all. I sold a microwave and some golf clubs. I sold a clothing iron and a lot of clothes. I sold camping gear and dishes and shoes.

I was left with one bowl, one cup, one fork, one knife. I learned how to live off a bag of rice, how to make twenty dollars last for two weeks, and how to scour the sidewalks for change underneath the parking meters. I learned to steal food and how to dress up and crash white-coat parties and weddings and graduations. I charmed dinner when I could and swiped apples when I couldn't. I ate dinner for free with the homeless men on Thanksgiving, cramming a to-go box and stretching those leftovers for a week.

On a desperately cold night in Vermont, I went to a crowded pub with the only friend I'd been able to make there, drank a one-dollar draft lager, and watched Barack Obama accept the presidency of the United States. Vermont was the first state to officially vote him in, and in ultra-liberal Burlington that night, boisterous, joyful crowds spilled out into the street. Students from UVM stripped to their naked skin and ran in snow boots down college street. Hope abounded.

My own life—fiscally, professionally, and emotionally—began a long, slow recovery that matched pace with that of our country. It was a better trip than the previous ride.

I'd moved to Arizona in the year 2000 with my husband, newlyweds who instantly got caught up in the materialism and patriotism of the new millennium. We were in the housing market before we even settled into our new jobs. And in the four years it took our marriage to fade, our house appreciated 140 percent. When we divorced, we sold it in seven hours, after a bidding war, and got ten grand more than our asking price. Those were the glory days of the Phoenix housing market.

I quickly built a house on my own, eagerly signing one of those ridiculous, inflatable, unreasonable mortgages that would prompt the housing bust. But in a twist that seems fortuitous in retrospect, I left Phoenix just as the wave was cresting, just before the bottom fell out and all my peers went bankrupt and foreclosed. That time, to sell my house I fretted for four months and took the first offer I got, for eight grand less than the asking price. When I first bought that house, there were four thousand houses available on the market across the valley. When I sold it, there were forty thousand. Whole neighborhoods went vacant and feral.

I got out just in time. But I was not prescient. It was not some real estate sophistication that prompted me to move out of Arizona. It was a dawning awareness that if I didn't leave the job, my fire department job, then I was going to commit suicide. Someone, somewhere, could be digging a grave for me. It's only now, over a decade later, in the birth and rapid convalescence of the #MeToo movement, that I have the stomach to look back objectively at the culture of that place. It was a place I fit into very well, until I dug my own grave.

Remember Fallen Brother*, Chief Bob Costello
who died at home on April 8, 2021, of cardiac arrest related
to Covid-19.

*R.F.B. is firefighter jargon equivalent to R.I.P.

#SheToo

How a woman in a man's world learned to harass
Anywhere, USA. Any time of year.

I worked as a firefighter, an EMT, a paramedic, and a dispatcher in the western United States. As a woman working in an over-whelmingly male environment, I learned to behave the same way the men did. I humped hose and I grabbed ass. I cheated on my spouse and I drank like a fish. I slept with everybody. I didn't do it to advance, but rather, to fit in. And fit in I did . . . until the day I didn't.

Like many men who take off a uniform, I wasn't quite sure what to wear after I left the profession. When I walked away from the job, I walked away from half my identity. It took years to figure out what kind of woman remained. Today, she wears a dress every day. And she waits for her own public reckoning. This chapter contains my reflections on that job, my own culpability, the pressure to conform, and the importance of due process.

The Salvage Tarp: Everyone Has an Angle

The gun in my mouth is a .22 caliber pistol. So if I can get the bullet in my head, through the roof of my mouth, it'll bounce around inside my skull. But if I miss, I'm fucked. If I hesitate on the trigger pull, or pull out just a little bit, I'll just blow the front of my face off. Too low, and I'll just hit the brain stem or the spinal cord, condemning myself to a vegetative or paralytic life. None of those options are acceptable. Nor, at this point, is life.

Those details don't deter me now as I walk with purpose toward my chosen kneeling place. I've worked it out before. Systematic. Cold. Most of my preparation is in deference to my family, my crew, and the first responders. It's not for me.

I stole a big red tarp off one of the out-of-service fire engines parked behind the station. It's the tarp we use to cover a family's belongings during a house fire, to limit smoke and water damage. It's called a salvage tarp. We also use it on multi-casualty incidents as a place upon which to cohort the injured for triage and treatment. And now it's hanging on the wall in my little one-bedroom generic apartment.

This is the apartment I came to when my infidelity ended my marriage. It's the apartment where I brought a thousand lovers, all brothers in the badge, and where I fucked my way through the ranks of all the neighboring fire departments: captains, battalion chiefs, assistant chiefs. It's where I learned that people either love me or hate me. No one is ambivalent. Now that they hate me, they don't want me around. Not like they did when they could fuck me.

And now it'll be the place where I spray my brains all over the wall, all over that stolen red tarp that still smells like the apparatus bay, nailed to the wall and draped on the floor. I've placed a business card on the kitchen counter for a trauma clean-up company. The door is unlocked, the keys to my car and to this apartment also resting on the counter. The car is clean and gassed, the title and registration inside it. The house is clean, the bed is made, and the laundry is done. The trash is empty. My advance directive and my funeral wishes sit on the counter. I have no plants that will need watering, no dog that will need to be fed. There will be no last-minute call for help.

Every day hurts so much that the thought of a bullet splitting my head in half sounds soothing. I've dressed in my neatly
pressed fire department uniform. It's not for work anymore. It's
for making a statement: "I don't know what else to wear. I'm naked without this."

Now, all that's left is the kneeling and the shooting. I walk
toward the tarp with purpose, careful and measured. I kneel, facing away from the tarped wall. I check the single bullet in the
chamber and release the safety. I bring the gun to my mouth and
put it between my teeth, looking in reverse down the barrel in
lining it up, from left to right and top to bottom. It feels hard and
cold between my incisors. My finger feels hot on the trigger more
so than the trigger feels cold. My knees feel hot where they press
into the floor, my heels hot on my ass where they're tucked, steel
toes digging into the ground. I drop my left arm and steady my
grip. Ready.

The Kitchen: Indoctrination

I don't remember which of their dicks I saw first. After a while,
they all start to look the same. I was no virgin when I took the job
and no stranger to foul language and dirty jokes. Those things
seem to come naturally to me. They have since the moment I put
on my first pair of steel-toed boots. I laugh at the dirty jokes because I find them funny. I curse because it helps me express the
powerful things I need to express. I think about sex as much as
the boys do, and in as much graphic detail. I watch pornography
too, because it turns me on.

The whole environment of the firehouse turns me on, maybe
despite or maybe because I'm a girl. Whatever it is, I feel very at
home in the station, a gruff, industrial place where the line between home and workplace is functionally blurred. We spend a
third of our lives there.

There are a lot of rooms in that municipal structure, but the basic building block of any firehouse includes the apparatus bay, or "the bay" for short. It's just a garage. Some are big and fancy, with twenty-foot roll-up doors of glass and aluminum and a wide-open floor, sloped for drainage and coated in slip-resistant paint that fends off grease and soot and blood. Others are as basic as a three-sided shed that barely keeps the sun and the rain off the truck. In California some of the bays have seismic sensors that automatically open the doors at the onset of an earthquake, so the rigs don't get stranded behind bent and lopsided door frames. Aircraft rescue and firefighting stations alongside the runway have thickly-insulated doors that prevent noise and jet wash and foreign object debris from overwhelming the crews who live there.

No matter where the garage is around the country, it smells like every other apparatus bay. It smells like faded diesel exhaust, off-gassing soot from piles of bunker gear, and a little bit of sweat. It smells like antiseptic wipes and testosterone and a whiff of last night's dinner. It smells like cheap coffee in a big metal pot and water in a big steel tank. It smells like tires and chrome polish, and I love it.

That smell, it does something to me. It makes me feel accepted as someone who proved her worth. And rejected as someone who was both too strong and too weak to do the job. The apparatus bay makes me feel masculine. I stand differently there, feet in a wide stance and arms crossed. Or, maybe, hands on hips. I walk differently there, the muscles of my chest puffed out into my blue shirt, polished boots clicking on the floor. Proud. I speak differently, both in cadence and in content. And I feel freer to think like a man, touch like a man, and fuck like a man.

There's another kind of door that leads out of the apparatus bay, aptly named a "man-sized" door. It's the same kind of door you'd find in your own house, and it serves the same function. Ingress. Egress. Transition between rooms.

Those doors lead to the kitchen, the cascade room, the day room, the bunk room, the bathroom, the gym, the dining room, the offices, the "house" part of the firehouse. Given that we all live together, the line between home and work is poorly demarcated, both functionally and emotionally. For better or for worse, we're all there together. Some crews are tight, close-knit. Others are fractured and feudal, just like any family.

There's a kitchen. On a good day, there's enough time for the crew to go grocery shopping. In most places, people pay into a "shift kitty." We pay a set amount for dinner (on my crew, it was seven bucks). That pooled money follows the crew to the grocery store, where often a half-full cart gets abandoned in the aisle when a call kicks out. If our shopping was interrupted, the staff would usually tuck our half-full cart into the back room, refrigerated, and await our return.

One of my favorite meals to cook, with one of my mentors, was chicken parmesan. It was a lengthy process, but we had a system, he and I. It was a time of ease, a time of laughter, a time for the two of us to share things. I felt safe then. He was the captain, but he was young in that role. I trusted him because of our time in that kitchen.

On chicken parm night, I'd start by making the batter mixture: breadcrumbs, spices, pepper, and a touch of flour. He'd be trimming the chicken breasts and preparing the oil in the skillet. Oven at 350°, I'd beat the eggs and milk in a big glass bowl. There's a mantra for young firefighters, "We pump at one fifty, cook at three fifty, and eat at twelve and five."

"One fifty" refers to the PSI of water pumped by the engine as it's filling up the hose. "Three fifty" is the generic oven temperature we teach the young men, many of whom cook their first formal meals in the firehouse. And the mealtimes are part of the militaristic regiment upon which the fire service in America is modeled. There's a chain of command. There is standardized training. And there are rites of passage like learning to cook for a crew of ten.

While my captain was frying the breaded chicken breasts, I used a big cheese slicer to pull off long, thin strands of provolone from the block we'd gotten at the grocery. He never let me buy the pre-sliced stuff. I suppose it was one of his many small tests of my willingness to obey the chain of command. We'd slide everything in the oven and get ready to set the table with big oval ceramic plates and hard plastic cups. But before we got to that, we had a special thing, just for the two of us.

He'd save the little odd pieces of chicken that didn't constitute a real serving portion, and he'd fry them up for us, a little reward for our work. We'd top it with a little chunk of provolone, the odd ends that I'd left behind, dip them in the marinara on the stove, and munch on them. The other guys would be in the gym, or taking a nap, or working on paperwork, or washing their pickups out behind the bay. I'd have a moment of respite with no one else around to judge me or nitpick me or ridicule me.

Later, in a different room, in a different station, my captain failed me. He watched the others crucify me and never said a word. All those hours sautéing and stirring and laughing together evaporated like the steam over the pasta pot. Our brotherhood became as fleeting as those tiny stove fires we occasionally put out for each other. He watched me get roasted and never had the balls to turn down the heat.

The Cascade Room: Cornered

There was a room toward the back of the station that was poorly lit, poorly ventilated, and always hot as hell. In it was an industrial ice machine that was constantly churning and compressing and belching out reams of ice cubes. It kicked out a constant flow of mechanized hot air. One of the tricks the guys would play on the booter (the rookie) would be to tell him to go circulate the ice. "You know, bring the ice at the bottom to the top, and the ice on the top to the bottom . . . so it doesn't get stale."

So some poor kid, trying to do his best, would be out there half the night with the ice scooper, right hand red and aching, scooping over and over, trying to get all the ice off the bottom of the unit. It was a ridiculous task and one of many games we played. In the good times, on the good crew, those were fun. In other places, those games were demeaning and hurtful.

Next to the ice machine stood the "cascade system," three large green tanks filled with oxygen. Each was as tall as my shoulders and connected to the others by a high-pressure hose encased in a flexible steel mesh. This was the place to refill the portable oxygen canisters we carried on the ambulance. After every few calls, at least once or twice per shift, it was my job to "fill the Os."

It would often be two or three in the morning, when the rest of the crew was already back in bed and I was so exhausted that my eyelashes hurt. All I wanted to do was crawl into bed like everyone else. But I had an obligation to the next patient. So I'd half stumble into the cascade room, close off and bleed the little O_2 tank, and unscrew the regulator. Pick up the bottle, mount it onto the cascade line. Use the key to crack it open. Then, in sequence, open and close the three big tanks to gently fill, then pressurize, the little one. It would change temperature in my hand in response to the compression of gas inside it.

The Cascade Room was a logical place to corner me and whip out a dick. I didn't resist. Early on, I got a lot of attention as a young woman. These men I admired, these men I aspired to be, these men to whom I attributed idol status, when they looked at me with hunger I took it as a compliment. It felt good to be desired, to be seen. It was addictive. I missed it if it wasn't there, like I was missing an essential part of me, an essential part of my worth.

I looked at all of their dicks. I touched a few. And I kept them hard, all the time. It was such a part of my day that I should've put it on my curriculum vitae.

The Bathroom: The Stench of It All

Ours was an older station that was built before there were many women in the profession. It didn't bother me. It felt authentic. And it was an unsterilized, unequalized, physical reminder that I was entering a world that had developed without the intention of having me in it. Not that it was exclusive of my gender purposefully, it just hadn't been a consideration in the architecture. There was not a precedent need for divided bunkrooms and separate bathrooms.

My bathroom in that station had originally belonged to the chief. It was on the opposite side of the bay from the bunkroom and the "gang shower" that belonged to the men. It was small, with an RV-sized shower in it, and it became the women's bathroom. There were only a few of us. It was small, cramped, with a few skinny lockers crammed into it. And we still had to share it with the chief.

As a booter, cleaning the station was a big part of the daily responsibility, especially the bathroom, especially the toilet. Strict shift captains would place a penny under the seat so they could check on whether you'd really cleaned it. Sneaky captains would place one on the base of the toilet, at the very back, to see if you'd really scrubbed the whole thing, top to bottom. Mean guys would purposefully have a bowel movement in there instead of the other bathroom, just so I'd have to smell their rancid feces while I was completing my chores. Sometimes they didn't flush. Once someone did it in the holding tank, an "upper-decker" they called it.

One of the chiefs would always leave his dirty underwear in that bathroom. I didn't think it was meant as an insult, but it was emblematic of a man and a profession and a generation. He'd leave them, replete with smears of stool and dribbles of yellow urine, draped over the handicap bar next to the toilet. Right in front of my face as I sat to urinate.

I'd clean the whole bathroom from top to bottom, even taking a ladder off the truck to clean off the tops of the lockers I couldn't reach, even using the brass polish and a rag to shine the doorknob, but I wouldn't touch those shorts.

I would've thought that after several years of sharing a bathroom, after decades of sensitivity training, and with a respectable wife and daughter at home, that at some point he would have realized how rude and unprofessional his behavior was. But he didn't. Myself, I'd have been mortified had any of the guys seen my dirty underwear, even though mine were consistently free of urine and stool.

It wasn't until years later, when the chief burst into the dayroom at midnight, clad only in flip-flops and tighty-whiteys, intent upon scolding the late-night crew, that he would have his moment of awareness. The guys were probably playing video games or watching baseball, maybe laughing at a movie, and their volume got away from them. Chief burst in.

"Hey!"

"Shut the fuck up, it's midnight you cocksuckers!"

Four heads swiveled his way, popcorn or chewing tobacco hanging half-out of mouths, surprised. A few moments of silence and someone turned down the TV.

"Uh, Chief," said one brassy firefighter. "It's hard to take you seriously when you have piss marks on the front of your BVDs."

His gaze went down to his crotch. He turned on his heel, stormed back to his office, and crawled into his bunk. The next shift, there was no underwear on the handicap bar to stare me down or make me cringe. It was gone. I guessed he'd had his "pee too" moment.

I don't hold it against him. I didn't then. I don't now. We were just some people doing a job we'd been trained to do, trying to live up to the legacy of September 11 and being graded by a heroism that wasn't us. We did our best. Sometimes we failed. We failed in little ways that only hurt us, and we failed in big ways that hurt people. We hurt our crews, our families, our friends, and our patients.

There was another chief, one I didn't know well but respected immensely, who killed himself some years later. I don't think his death was ever technically ruled a suicide, but those of us who knew things knew that it was. I know what that last night of his probably looked like, what it felt like. I'd been there too.

That chief had been in a light duty position, recovering from some little injury or another. And he'd been overseeing the vehicle maintenance part of things. My rig had broken down that day, right in the middle of an emergency response. And as the booter, I had to wait for the tow truck and switch out the equipment to the backup rig. It was hot out. He'd stopped by to check on me while he was on his way home.

Hours later, the backup rig in service, dinner completed, ready to turn down my bunk and retire from my daily chores, the phone rang. An announcement came over the intercom for the whole station to hear.

Squelch . . .

"Booter! . . . Chief's on the phone!"

Squelch, static, silence.

I picked up an extension, leery, worried. The chief was calling to make sure I was okay. He wanted to make sure I had everything I needed, that I had eaten dinner and was back at the house. I was caught off guard. Even my own crew didn't care that much.

"I just wanted to make sure we got things straightened out and that you're okay."

"Uh, yeah, Yes, Sir. Thanks, Chief. I'm good. I'm home. We're all set."

It wasn't just his thoughtfulness I found disconcerting, it was the slur. I could tell, even in our superficial relationship, that he was drunk. He was off-duty, a status in which we'd never interacted before. I'd never spoken to him at home before. And he was sideways. It wasn't off-putting. It was endearing. Brotherly. Paternal without being patronizing. Hearing him then was like a window into hearing myself in the future in those moments of despair. When I heard he'd died, I knew that he was me. We were the same.

Here in the present, when I feel the dark memories coming and I don't have the energy to fight them off and I dive down that rabbit hole of pity and sorrow, he pops in my head. Not enough to stop my occasional binge drinking, but enough to make me think of the responders who could get called to my own death.

The cops and the medics and the firefighters, all my friends, would find me. I don't want them to find me face down in a pool of vomit. And I don't want them to find my underwear, in whatever state of repair, like I found the chief's. Those two men with brass on their shoulders weren't the same guy, but they wore the same shorts. I have no brass. I wear no shorts. But I don't want anyone to see my stains.

The Gym: A Singular Workout

Some years of my life I was very much into working out, hitting the gym, lifting weights, getting on the treadmill. But at the station, I wasn't one of the folks who was always in there. I was skittish about getting sweaty and tired and then having to run a call that required a lot of energy. Other guys didn't worry about that. If I was in the gym at the station, it was usually more of a social event.

So when I was accused of making out with a firefighter in the gym on duty, people were incredulous. Not about the making out part, but about my being in the gym. The next day, as I was getting off duty, the union president stopped by, meeting me just outside the bay, just outside the gym door.

I can remember the day clearly. The air was temperate, almost cool for that part of the country and that time of year. The sky was a clear robin's egg blue with the sharpness of morning and without the faintest of clouds to darken us. His words that followed, while I can't recall them verbatim, left me colder than I'd been before, even though I was sitting in the sun.

That brittle sky started to crack over my head, finely at first, in webs extending from the zenith toward the horizon, until the whole thing shattered with a deafening sound like crystal. Heavy blue chunks landed around me like giant summer hail. The roar of it left me ringing, a vice around my chest, and the sky above me now blacker than night, a void.

They were onto me. They could see through me. My job was on the line and I was the last one to know that my reputation in the industry was gone forever. Telephone, tell a friend, tell a fireman.

There was a black ball rolling down a slippery lane and it was aiming true. I'd have to tell my husband. I'd have to tell my friends. I'd have to tell my parents why I wasn't at work on the next A shift. That job, the dream, was disintegrating before me.

I looked down at the blue uniform shirt I was wearing and saw the cuffs unraveling, a single thread unwinding, all the way up the sleeves. My screen-printed name, perched above my left breast, began to peel away letter by letter, pieces of it wafting away on the breeze out of sight, the department logo following it. The pockets of my utility trousers grew heavy, as if they were filling with wet sand, pulling the waistband from my hips and crumpling on the ground at my feet. My boots, rubber-soled and steel-toed, quivered like jelly and melted away from my socks into the concrete.

I was left standing just outside the bay, relieved of my duties, exposed, in my bra and panties and sweat resistant socks. I was shivering, nearly naked. I crossed my legs, crossed my arms, lowered my head, and hunched my shoulders as all naked women do. And I just wanted to run. But this thing could not be outrun. No matter which direction I went, there were sure to be roadblocks waiting. And running toward them, naked, I'd be outmatched. Because that time I'd spent in the gym hadn't been on the treadmill.

The Captain's Office: Old Habits Die Hard

One of my captains tried to warn me early. He wasn't on my shift, but I saw him almost every day. He was just as naughty as me, though he had learned to restrain the most outward displays of it, a nod to his promoted status. He, like a lot of others in that department, had promoted early, young. He laughed and flirted the same as I did.

We were so much alike that he could see where I was headed, which was nowhere good. He understood that I was just trying to fit in, trying to play the role, play along. But he knew that people were already talking. For some reason, he cared enough about me to warn me. So he pulled me, literally by the hand, into his office and shut the door.

I realized, when his joviality dissipated, that I was in trouble. But I also knew I was safe. I knew, as he counseled me, that he cared about my well-being. He was coming from a place of love and concern, not of scorn, judgement, or rank-compelled duty. We sat knee-to-knee and he told me to watch my "six," to watch behind me. He counseled me to clean up my speech, tone down my sexual references, and recognize that the firehouse telegraph is the fastest in the West. He reminded me that as the new girl I needed to toe the line.

We didn't go into detail. We didn't talk about the idea that my behavior was no different than the guys. We didn't talk about our colleagues who'd been caught, investigated, and negligently retained for far worse offenses than just having a big mouth. We couldn't yet, at that time, talk about the people from our department who would go on to commit suicide or the others who would attempt it. We couldn't yet talk about the guy among us who would go off his meds and hold his family hostage, keeping the SWAT team at bay for hours and wielding an axe he'd taken off the fire truck.

We couldn't talk about those things because they hadn't happened yet. We talked instead about how I should edit myself. I heard him. Honestly. Fully. And it made me uncomfortable. In my immaturity, I was poorly equipped to deal with my own inadequacies. I sat across from that kindred spirit and felt my mask cracking. I responded with an act that, to the present day, I can't believe I did. I can't believe it was me. It was almost compulsive, reflexive. My cheeks still redden with shame when I recall it.

We were completing our discussion and had risen from our chairs, ready to move toward the door. He offered me a hug. It was not lewd. It was completely wholesome and brotherly. And I quickly moved into it, understanding the sentiment. He was a guardian of mine. And there, in the captain's office, in a moment that could not have lasted more than three seconds, I embraced him like a brother, and then lowered my right hand to grab a handful of his butt. A quick pinch of a navy-blue-clad cheek and I jumped back laughing.

He pushed me away, exasperated. "What . . . did I just . . . say?"

I giggled, awkward, a Cheshire Cat grin on my face, and ran out of the office, through the day room, and out into the bay, where I cast about, unsure of what to do or where to put my hands. I was befuddled by myself.

Eventually, I pulled on a pair of latex gloves, grabbed a garbage bag, and went out behind the station to collect hundreds of discarded cigarettes. It was an expected duty for any booter, and one that I loathed, since I didn't smoke. But on that day it seemed an appropriate penance, for most of those butts were his.

The Administration Building: Drinking Coffee

I sat on the edge of my seat in the administration building of the fire department, squaring off against a cadre of neatly pressed uniforms bearing surly faces. It was a tribunal of sorts, with a couple of chiefs and an HR professional, all firing off questions about my behavior, my motivation, my accomplices:

"Robin, did you kiss anyone in the gym while you were on duty?"

"No."

"Did anyone kiss you?" From the woman in the room.

"No."

"Robin, just who are you trying to protect?"

"Myself, Sir."

It went on for an hour. I was a booter, a rookie. I was on probation. That meant I could be fired without cause. I could lose my job for any reason. And they were ready to tell me to pack my things. I hadn't hurt a patient. I hadn't stolen anything from the station. I hadn't lied on my application, forged my certifications, or gotten a DUI. I hadn't shown up late for shift. I hadn't disobeyed the chain of command. I hadn't failed to complete a run report or failed a drug test.

What I had done was jump through all the union tradition hoops to get the job. I'd pounded signs and knocked on doors for political candidates endorsed by the International Association of Firefighters. I'd poured Kool-Aid for kids after leading their station tours. I wore a union shirt and walked a leg of the Relay for Life. I'd cleaned the union hall. I had come to the station with tubs of ice cream for hundreds of hours of ride-alongs, and I'd washed thousands of dishes. I'd sat through interview coaching sessions, though I could have taught them. I'd sat through fire science associates degree courses, though I already had the only bachelor's degree on the department.

I sailed through a written test and sat through the interview board, regurgitating the buzz words they'd taught me, more a parrot than a real candidate. And I got the job. I brought breakfast the first day, like they'd taught me. I showed up well over an hour early for every shift. I made sure I was the first one awake, every morning, starting the coffee before anyone else was up. I cleaned the station incessantly, even polishing the copper doorknobs and taking a toothbrush to the diamond plate on the truck. I ran to answer the phone every single time it rang. I never sat in the recliner chairs. I read the SOP book after dinner every night, a good student. I learned to spit-shine my boots. I picked up thousands of cigarette butts from around the station grounds. I took relentless criticism.

And one day, I stared in horror at a picture posted in the dining room of a woman soldier at the Abu Ghraib prison. She had a prisoner on all fours in a dog collar, leading him on a leash. It was a famous photograph. Someone had printed it from the internet and written our names, mine and the guy I was accused of kissing, above the figures on the photograph. They taped it on the whiteboard where it couldn't be missed. I ripped it down, tore it up, and threw it in the trash. Then I dutifully carried that trash out to the dumpster, like a good booter, choking down vomit and fighting back tears.

I had worked my ass off trying to do all the right things, trying like hell to fit in. And in the dark of night, they seemed to like it, my foul mouth, my dirty mind, my tolerance of the jokes and the games. They liked it when they cornered me in the cascade room so I could appraise what was in their pants. They liked it when they had their hands down my fly or up my uniform shirt. They liked it when they were with me on their off days and the other crews were lying to their wives, telling them they were working overtime.

But on that Monday morning with the polished brass in the admin building, none of that "boys will be boys, even if they're girls" stuff seemed to carry any weight. None of the guys spitting tobacco and adjusting their balls and asking me to cover for them when their wives called were there with me.

Not the battalion chief who mentored me but also wrestled with me, and then one day, put me over his knee and spanked me hard. The fingers of his other hand were fully into the seam of my uniform pants, pressing into my vulva, rubbing my clitoris.

My partner had noticed, but he hadn't stopped the chief. And he hadn't told anybody.

Not the captain, who used to tell me about how, every morning, he had anal sex with his wife in the kitchen while she poured the Lucky Charms for his kids. Not the firefighter who proselytized to me about God and then stroked himself to orgasm in the front seat of the ambulance while he was on an overtime shift with me. Not the paramedic who told me how much he fantasized about performing fellatio on another man with me. Not the guy who used to hold me down and tickle me until I peed. Not the crew who strapped me to a backboard in the apparatus bay and covered me with ketchup and relish and a bag of flour, then left me there when our house got toned out for a call.

None of those guys presented themselves as character witnesses at the tribunal. I sat virtually alone, feeling tiny, disempowered, and naked in the sterility of that office. Gone was all the hard work of doing the job itself. Gone were all the swinging dicks. And here instead were a team of people who got to sleep in their own bed every night and never had to watch anyone die. These were professionals who saw this job as a profession, not a way of life, not a family, not an identity.

They were there to tell me I couldn't have it anymore. I could no longer have a life I'd felt born into. I could no longer have that family who had made me laugh, watched me sleep, fed me, and clothed me. I'd have to take that badge down from where it had anchored my name. I now stood accused.

But there was one man there on my side. He sat to my left, and he had the advantage of looking the part. He fit the image of the most pious, most fit, most patriotic, and most flawless of us. He was my union rep, he was a veteran, and I'd seen his penis. We didn't talk about his penis that day. Instead, he flashed that unintimidated smile and said, "We have a labor-management agreement in this institution, and she deserves the benefit of due process. It's one person's word against another person's word, and we can't know the motivations of the woman who accused her."

The rest of the meeting has blurred in my memory, but there were discussions of written reprimands, sensitivity training, extended probation, and a graduated disciplinary plan. I kept my job, such as it remained. Though I still loved the work itself, the days were no longer fun. But I still woke up first and made the coffee.

The Dining Room: A Hurricane and a Glass House

It was late that night, more than twelve hours after I'd started my twenty-four-hour shift. The job had become brutal. The volume of calls hadn't changed, nor had the nature of them. The four walls of the firehouse hadn't changed, nor had the layout of the rooms in them. But after my hand-spanking and reprimanding, I'd been trying to navigate a new identity in an old familiar place. I was trying to edit myself the way I'd been coached. People didn't respond well to it. All of a sudden, no one knew how to take me or how to approach me. And I wasn't sure how to approach myself.

Then Hurricane Katrina happened. In the desert, no one had previously cared about any hurricane. It was too far away to have any impact, and the idea of too much water in such a parched land was completely foreign. It was an amount of death, destruction, and disruption for which we had absolutely no frame of reference. I remember watching the coverage on the news. And I remember watching the people around me (almost all men, almost all White, almost all Christian, almost all uneducated in a formal academic sense) disintegrate. They turned from the respectable, if imperfect, men I knew into monsters.

Racism, in its basest, most unsophisticated, most virulent permutation, took off its civil mask and roared unprovoked through our civil servant house. As footage of floating Black bodies coursed across Fox News, people around me talked of ethnic cleansing. As turkey vultures picked at a dog carcass on CNN, men in blue uniforms called Black people "human pigeons." There was laughter at families stranded on an overpass or a rooftop. The N-word was used to describe a son wading through thigh deep water with his dead Black mother in his arms.

On the first night, I was shocked. I tried to hold my tongue. Finally, at the dinner table, shame burning my face, I implored, "Guys, can you ease up on the 'pigeon' talk please?"

That's all it took. They saw my weak point. From there opened an ethnocentric floodgate, day after day, shift after shift, week after week of the interminable rescue and recovery effort along the gulf coast. They knew it got to me, so they kept at it, denigrating a whole race of Americans, despite the noble oath they'd sworn.

They couldn't seem to understand why I cared so much.

"You're not Black."

"What, is your mom Black or something?"

"What, do you have a Black best friend?"

I didn't have the vocabulary to reason with people who clearly, utterly, did not share a sense of humanity that was just inherent in me. I didn't know how to tell them racism was wrong.

At first, I asked them to stop. Then I tried to reason with them. They turned it back on me; if I could be inappropriate, then so could they. It was a race to the bottom. I'd find quotes scribbled on the whiteboard. "People in glass houses shouldn't throw rocks."

Then I just turned silent. I started walking away. They'd push the line further and further, until I left the room. I left dinners uneaten, returning when everyone else was finished to dutifully wash the dishes and clean the kitchen. I'd retire to my bunk early or work on something in the office on the computer. And I started writing, not about the things that were going on, but about life and the job itself. There were things I couldn't carry around in my head anymore, not if I was to shoulder all this other junk.

People grew more and more suspicious of me. They seemed to be more and more afraid of where my protests would eventually lead. Then came the night of the inquisition.

It was late that night, more than twelve hours after I'd started my twenty-four-hour slog. Over the intercom came, "Robin, come to the dining room."

That couldn't be good. I walked delicately into the dining room, an open space that was contiguous with the day room, full of Firehouse magazines, spit cups, and a giant screen TV. The whole crew was there waiting for me. Five of them, waiting for one of me. A hard, wooden chair was turned around in its place, backed up against the dining room table. In front of it, arrayed like a poker hand, were five recliners. Each faced inward, a spoke to the hub of my chair. And over each was draped a man or woman in blue, their feet propped up in socks and flip-flops.

"Have a seat."

I stepped warily to the place that had clearly been set for me. The next two hours were a blur. A barrage of insults and putdowns came at me in that chair like I was a John McEnroe contestant. A fist full of reprimands. Teeth full of scorn. A few highlights stuck out and could be distilled into, "No one likes you and we want you to bid off the shift."

In that time, I went from sitting upright, to shoulders stooped and hands in my lap, to tears welling in my eyes. Once those tears began to fall, an incoherent torrent followed, my Irish face red, swollen, blotchy, and snotty. At some point, late into the night, my face raw from the crying, a battalion chief walked in, odd for that late. He surveyed the incident and asked, "So, uh, what's going on?"

Poker faces from my crew. Silence from me.

"We're just talkin' Chief."

"Okay."

He eyed me, sitting there trying to relax my shaking shoulders, sniff the snot from my face, and suppress my burgeoning hiccups.

"Okay. Be safe guys. Goodnight."

He dropped a stack of papers on the table and left. The barrage resumed until it had reached whatever goal they'd previously set. And at some point they released me. I stumbled to the far side of the station, across the apparatus bay, and out into the desert night, distraught. I paced back and forth for a long time, trying to get myself under control, trying to reconcile the loss of illusion, the loss of a belief in an institution, the loss of belief in heroes.

Eventually my captain, the one with whom I'd cooked a thousand dinners, came outside to tell me he was taking me off the truck for the night. It wasn't inappropriate. I'd have put myself out of service if he hadn't. He stood there in front me, in my deepest distress, and showed his cowardice.

"I kind of felt like the guys went too far. I mean, they don't want you on this shift, but I don't think they needed to go that far."

My tears instantly dried and fury rose from my navel to my chest to my throat. "Then why didn't you stop them?" I asked.

There was no answer. Not that night. Not all the other nights. Not from any anybody. And I never talked about it, not to my family, not to my friends, not to the administration, nor an attorney. I didn't fight that fight for the same reasons other people don't. I was up against an institution. I was up against a way of life, a tradition, a national symbol spray painted in patriotism and chanting the new songs of the blossoming War on Terror. I was up against the American flag. How do you stand and fight against an enemy you still love, against a man you still consider your friend? How do you hand back a badge you still so badly want?

Shortly after that night, some of those same guys were selected, in preference over me, for deployment to Louisiana. They went to Jefferson Parrish and St. Bernard and all the others, all the places where 1,245 people died and 135 were never found. Some of those dudes pulled in a hundred grand that year, rescuing the "Niggers" they'd been laughing at from 1,500 hundred miles away.

I bid off the shift.

The Man-Sized Door: Freedom

Eventually, years later, I decided, of my own free will, to leave that place. It had become too toxic and had taken away everything I thought I needed to live. At the end of my last shift, I packed up my bed linens, my spare boots, the stuff from my locker, and my stethoscope, and I walked out the man-sized door one last time. No one walked me out. And I didn't look back.

I met the big chief, the one from the tribunal, for coffee at a café down the street on the morning after my last shift. He'd asked for the meeting. Since the dust had largely settled and the department had moved on to other drama, he wanted my perspective. He wanted to know what had really happened.

I opened up to him, and he to me. I told him the details of how I'd almost killed myself with a .22 on a tarp I'd stolen off the truck. He seemed glad that I hadn't. I told him about how, out of 150 guys I worked with over the years, probably 30 of them showed me their cocks. And that the odd thing was, at the time, I didn't think it was odd. I thought it meant I was one of the guys.

He told me about how quickly he had ascended the ranks. About how he'd done all the right things, played the right game. About how he fit the exact mold of this place, but how he regretted that he never got to have an experience like mine. He was never carefree in a lower rank, without the burden of responsibility. He was never free to participate in the fun and games, never really included in the family of a crew, because he grew out of it so quickly. He envied my freedom to walk away without those brass handcuffs on my wrist.

I drank my latte in that light of an easier Monday morning and grinned with the freedom of a woman who had nothing to lose. I walked away and left him there, left them all there, dark knowledge and black coffee staining teeth once so white.

A Flash in the Pan: An Afterword for Moving Forward

As I've purged myself of these unflattering secrets to myself, my family, my colleagues, and the world, I find that what remains is a dearth of vocabulary to explain our shared MeToo history and our shared path forward. There are psychologists, sociologists, biologists, and anthropologists who are better equipped to discuss that movement in educated detail, and we should be counting on them, among others, to design our forward-looking roadmap. But there are a few points that I offer for reasonable, empathetic, and open-minded discussion.

Don't rape. There is a difference between assault and harassment. There are no gradations of rape, there is consent or no consent. There are, however, gradations of harassment, and the assessment of severity lies in the eyes of both the harassed and the adjudicators. Those could be an employer, a risk manager, an arbitrator, a judge, or a jury. To an overweighted extent these days, the jury often includes the court of public opinion, which by nature is underinformed and biased. But assault is assault and it's never okay. We should teach men and women, boys and girls, not to assault each other.

Support our due process. You never know when you might need it. In the words of *Hustler* founder Larry Flynt: "If [it] will protect a scumbag like me, then it will protect all of you. Because I'm the worst." I believe in the value of union representation. The union, into which I enrolled voluntarily and to which I gladly contributed dues, ensured that I had a fair hearing, a chance to speak, and the benefit of time, correction, and due process. In their enforcement of my remediation, they invested in our shared future. To that end, I have striven to make them proud and to develop into the kind of professional that is worthy of their efforts. But I have been fallible in that quest.

Elect, hire, and advance women. If we're going to start a robust conversation in our society about what the rules and expectations are going to be, then lots of differing perspectives will be important. Diversity is valuable. Hire women of different nationalities, races, abilities, and levels of education. Educate them. Promote them. Elect them. Appoint them. And insist that they participate openly with men in this conversation. Women, stop tearing other women down. We all lose.

Ask your mother. She knows a lot. Daughters, talk to your mothers. Daughters, talk to your grandmothers. Try to understand how different her life was, in comparison with yours, and revel in the progress we've made. It's okay to continue to celebrate your great-grandmother's victory while working toward your own. Don't let the imperfection of our journey be the enemy of the good we're all doing. Men, talk to your mothers, too. And then to your daughters. Girls, celebrate the men in your life who celebrate you, believe in you, and stand up for you.

Jerk off. Before you make any major decision in life, masturbate. It works. Our sexual strategies as a species are deeply integrated into everything we do. There are irrepressible drives, for men and women both that are part of the very fabric of us. Denying that will worsen the outcome and suppress literate conversation. I make a studied effort to express my desires outside the workplace, so that I may remain professionally distant. I submit that other men and women can do the same. After all, like Larry Flynt, I'm one of the worst, but I'm hardly alone.

The Iron Mountain and the Mur-écran

Social engineering that has survived the downturn
Fermont, Quebec. A different winter.

Four years and two jobs pass between when I first set out on the road toward Fermont and when I actually arrive. I was derailed a thousand times, but eventually I make it. As soon as I get off the plane, I hop in a taxi and go straight to the "wall," to the "wind screen." The "Mur-écran" embodies, in one space, everything else I've found along the way. Shelter, community, purpose, entertainment, pride, and generational sustainability. Fermont, next to the Mont-Wright iron mine, was built as the mining town of the future, to combat the destructive culture of temporary and transient work. The wind screen was built to shield the town. And for forty years, it has worked.

Walking through the "wall," there's not much to see. The corridor of the Mur-écran is sparse, stoic, and still. Off to one side, there are short, switch-backed stairways that lead up to small landings, flanked by steel apartment doors. Beneath them, and alongside, another half-flight of steps curves downwards. In less than ten steps, they dead-end at another apartment door. Most of the stair treads are diamond plate steel, though some are wooden, open between the planks. The handrails are stout pieces of blond 2" x 6" wood, heavily varnished against forty years of hands. They are supported on thin, square, steel rods. The rods are painted brown, just like the landings and most of the apartment doors.

Small wooden plaques, in that same varnished blond, are used to display both an apartment number and a painted animal. The animal icon could be an elk, a rabbit, a bear, a fox, or a squirrel. I'm not sure why the squirrel. It's not the most robust of arctic animals, especially since there are moose here in far Northern Quebec, on the border with Labrador. Perhaps the original artist who selected these figures was a Rocky and Bullwinkle fan, and chose a subtle bait and switch, moose to squirrel, in his art.

The Mur-écran (French for wind screen) of Fermont, Quebec, is composed of several sections that, on first review, seem as though they could have been built in different years. In fact, the entirety of the town was built at the same time. It's not a straight line. One can't look from the east end to the west end uninterrupted. The wall warps upon itself, forming a protective cup around the north end of the town of Fermont. A walk along the corridor, 1.3 kilometers, is not a straight march. There are long stretches that dead-end into ninety degree "right-flank-right" vestibules, which themselves lead on to continuing hallways.

Some of those intersections contain the main access doorways into the wall. They are recognizable from the outside as electric orange towers of standing-seam steel. Other corners offer a half-height window into the gray, snowy, windward side of the wall. The floors are some indiscriminate brown linoleum that is curiously unbroken, even for long lengths. Here and there, at the junctions, there are down-going steps, four or five apiece, with non-skid rubber and more of those varnished blond wood handrails.

In the center sections of the Mur, the ceilings are quite high, two stories at least. They are equal in height with the interior ceilings of the two-bedroom bachelor apartments that are behind the brown doors. In other places, the ceiling is quite close, seven feet, I'd guess, and faced with wooden planks the likes of which you'd see inside a sauna or a steam room. Along still other corridors, there are industrial dropped ceilings to hide wiring and ductwork for the HVAC system. Those air handlers are an important part of the experience of the wall.

As soon as I check in at the front desk of the only hotel in Fermont, the sad and outdated Hotel Fermont, I learn that my room is a few minutes away from being ready to occupy. But I can't wait any longer. I've known about this place for so long. I've read of it, listened to it, and seen pictures of it for years now.

No one cares as much about this place as a sociological experiment and item of fascination as I do, unless they've lived here. The Mur-écran has elevated over the years in my mind to a thing of fantasy, a dream world, the way the Statue of Liberty or Mount Rushmore does for an American school child.

I hired a taxi to bring me here from the tiny airport in Wabush, Labrador, twenty miles away. On that snowy, gray trip, I'd shared the reason for my visit with the taxi driver, a native Labradorean who seemed to respect that I was writing about this chunk of the world. There aren't a lot of visitors to this corner of North America. There are no tourists except for the occasional motorcyclist looping the Trans-Labrador highway.

When we came over the crest of a black spruce, snow-laden hilltop and I could see the wall for the first time, my breath caught in my throat. Here was this fantastical thing, this weird thing, in front of me in real life. Without my prompting, the driver pulled off the main road into a little turnabout, a spot with a view of the town below, where the mining company has parked one of those big haul trucks as a display. A gigantic version of a child's Tonka toy, the dump truck had a small park built around it and was outlined in small white lights for the approaching Christmas.

I'll see it later, in the twilight, from the far end of the wall, and I'll wonder at where I am, what I'm doing, why I'm here.

To get there, I start at the hotel, the eastern end of the Murécran. And I walk. And walk. And walk. I'm wearing calf-high snow boots and wind-proof pants that swish when my legs pass each other. I wear a puffy undercoat and a backpack, carrying in my arms my street boots, my hat and gloves, and my heavy overcoat. For ten minutes on a Saturday morning, I walk alone. I let the linoleum and the brown paint and the blond wood and the straight corners and the fluorescents wash over me.

I smell it, mostly sterile, less musty than one would expect of 1971. But what I really swim through is the sound. I want more of it. So much so that after I drop my stuff in the hotel room, I change out of the clunky snowshoes and swishy wind pants into a comfortable dress, a pair of tights, and the only other shoes I have, a pair of black leather, ankle-high, square-heeled, lug-soled boots. And I walk again.

Now it's Saturday afternoon. The middle portion of the wall, replete with bachelor apartments, also houses the commercial center. It looks like any Midwest-America mall. And here in December, it's strung with Christmas tinsel. Santa has come calling, and the whole place has been turned into a winter wonderland for toddlers. And toddle they do, in tiny snowsuits and tousled blond hair, speaking tiny French. I find the fake snow ironic.

A man drives a tiny train around and around in the center portion of the wall, giving rides. Inside a blow-up igloo downstairs, Santa and an imp of an elf pick up snotty kid after snotty kid. I amble past and through all that motion and commotion and out across the shoulders, arms, and wrists of the embracing wall. The farther I walk, the more the sounds return to the norm, the farther they get from the manufactured "Polar Express" of strollers and screams, baby bumps and baby bibs.

Out at the fringes, in the wrists and the fingers of this thing I've personified, everything is closed. The town offices at the west end will remain empty until Monday. All I can see through the wired glass is a dark municipal office with, again, a switch-backed stairwell going down to what I presume is the firehouse, based upon the way it looks from the exterior. Oddly, on a little corkboard in the stairwell, there is a suicide prevention poster hanging. It's somewhat generic, so I guess that it's targeted toward Canadians in general, not Fermonters in particular.

I walk to the extreme end of the wall, and it abruptly stops at a locked fire-resistant door. The door separates the Mur-écran and its living spaces from the town library and the school. A sign, in French, warns of the importance of keeping this door closed and locked outside normal business hours.

When my feet stop, a silence descends like fat, fluffy snow-flakes on a deep windless night. It falls over me like a shawl, the stillness. I stand for a moment, looking back the way I came, up the linoleum hall, where there's no one. Then, like a veil, the un-earthly silence slowly lifts. There's a breathing, a breath, to this place. It's a soft hum of warm air through galvanized steel air han-dlers. There's a thin buzz of overhead fluorescents, louder in some places than others. Weaker in those corridors that are dressed with sauna-wood on the ceiling. It's the background soundtrack to this place, to the town.

Outside there's constant movement, even on the stillest of days. There's a panoply of clouds, changing quickly. It's like watch-ing a landscape painted upon a scroll, rolled from left to right by some giant hand. There's the ever-setting sun, ever-rising, just barely hovering over the southern horizon, slanting the light for a few hours before disappearing for most of the day. There are hardy winter birds, rapid in their flight and high pitched in their screeching, protesting against the cold. There are crunching snow boots and spiked tires and the familiar pause and puff of yellow school bus exhaust.

Then there's the inexorable wind. It's a wind that piles the snow and wipes the ice and plummets the thermometer. It's a wind that scrunches shoulders and clenches fists and grits teeth. It's the wind that created the wall that created the town that created the community that persists to this day.

Inside the wall, I can open my fists, relax my shoulders, and unclench my teeth. I can open my mouth wide enough to talk to the people here, united in purpose and commiserating in the cold. Inside the wall it's silent, except for the warmth of air and the sizzle of light.

I walk back the way I came, through the chlorine around the Olympic-sized pool, past the noisy St. Nick crowd, beyond the next main entrance corner and into the eastern barrens of the Mur-écran. Again, there's only that soft humming and the rhythmic tapping of my boots. Somewhere, in the minutes and minutes of walking, a door opens and closes. A pair of feet starts away from me. That's all. Nothing else.

I look behind me, then in front, trying to find the source of that human sound, but it's beyond my angled field of view. Later I smell perfume, intense, as though a woman has just passed, but there's been no door sound, no marching of feet, no conversation, nothing to betray where she's come from or where she's gone. Other than that, in this scent-neutral wintertime, there is almost no smell. Nothing cooking. Nothing baking. No flowers. No warm laundry. Just the salinity of snow and cold and plows. And the sterility of linoleum.

But beyond that sterility, there is warmth and light and community and protection. There is collegiality and help. The helpers themselves live in the wall. The firefighters and the medics and the cops and the doctors and the nurses and the teachers. They are the protectors of us, the best of us, the future of us. And they live here in the wall. The Mur-écran is the fortress against cold and sickness and poverty and loneliness.

Fermont was not the first town here. First Nationers have hunted this area for moose and caribou and fowl for generations, though most of the permanent establishments of the Indigenous population are further north and east, along the coasts. That's common around the Arctic. In the wintertime, it's easier to travel across the frozen bays and fjords, as opposed to over the forested land.

The principal reason that modern people in the Americas have mushed their way inland is in the search for minerals. Here that mineral is iron. Iron Mountain. Fer (iron) mont (mountain). The inhospitable earth here is loaded with it, along with graphite, phosphate, nickel, lithium, and rare earths (used in smart phones and dirty bombs). Traditionally, mining companies have been good at setting up pop-up towns to house the mine workers on a semi-permanent basis. Pop-up towns have only what you need and nothing that you don't. They lack luxury. It's basic shelter, basic food, basic supplies, basic work. And base entertainment.

In these towns, there's always, if nothing else, a bar. The bar gets built as the first rudimentary housing foundations are being laid. And often, not always, a strip club comes closely on its heels. Boys will be boys but, more importantly, capitalists will be capitalists. Men and women have long known how to exploit the most basic of needs in the men who exploit the ground for its metal.

Sex, booze, and food. In a place where there is only work and money, there will always come the distractions of sex, booze, and food. Many a shrewd, if exploited, woman has made a living providing those. Fermont is no exception. In the Mur-écran, next to the hotel, next to the gift shop and sundry store, the dress shop, the winter outfitter, and the travel agency, one floor up from the only restaurant in town, the post office, the liquor store, the grocery store, and the movie theater, is the strip club.

The strip club is behind some porthole windows covered with black velvet curtains and has its own dark vestibule where a French placard tells me I should be prepared to show two forms of ID to prove I'm over eighteen. The first time I saw it, the toddlers of Saturday's Polar Express were milling about, eating cotton candy, and dropping popcorn on the floor. Families with teenagers stood just outside the door, but no one seemed bothered by it.

"Everybody goes to the club," my dinner waitress tells me with a sultry Quebecois accent. "If you want to take a beer or play the slot machines, it's okay. You just don't look at the girls."

The strippers are easy to pick out of the crowd. They're young and relatively thin, childless and relatively haggard. They can be found outside the door of the hotel smoking or beyond the parking garages smoking. They can also be found in the post office and the grocery and the restaurant next to everyone else. After all, there is nowhere else to go. Everything is here in the wall.

I've no need to see the strippers today, so I explore the center of the Mur-écran in more detail. There's a daycare, a laundromat, a dry cleaner, a hair salon, and a couple of clothing stores. Up a flight of stairs is a small radio station that broadcasts for a few hours a day, a few days a week, and has since the place was christened in the early '70s.

Large murals on the walls, made up of photographs and artists' renderings, give a history of the development of Fermont, "the Northern Mining Town of the Future." The 1969 drawings are an egalitarian vision of a future that is now more than three decades in the past. The architects and their illustrators drew up a utopia suited for the north.

In the sketches, Mary Tyler Moore women of voting freedom and work responsibilities and the pill stroll sophisticatedly through outdoor spaces of trees and promenades and urban landscaping. Children in bell bottoms and teenagers with mutton chops ride bicycles on paved streets, surrounded by green grass between modular homes of fresh wood and bright paint. Now, a decade and a half into the new millennium, the hallways of the Mur-écran are as woefully outdated as the bell bottoms and the Dorothy Hamel haircuts in the pictures. But, somehow, it's still sturdy and well-kept and aesthetically pleasing. The Mur has accomplished the dual goals of creating a leeward micro-climate to temper the bitter cold for the houses in its shadow and to create an envelope of community and connectivity.

Tucked safely inside the Mur-écran, workers became towns-people, then became friends. Soon, they became a family, irrevo-cably tied to their strange little northern home and to each other. Like most mining towns, until the trucks hit the bottom of the hole Fermont will continue to exist. But, in contrast to its neigh-bors, Fermont, with its signature wall, still thrives.

When the price of iron drops, so do the interconnected econ-omies of Northern Quebec and Labrador. The first people to leave this harsh environment when the money dries up are the fly-in/fly-out workers who are only tied to it by a paycheck and noth-ing else. Thus, the communities of Wabush and Labrador City are floundering, rusting, and peeling in the arctic twilight. Eighty percent of their population has left and most of the remainder is unemployed.

Fermont, as well, had a contingent of fly-ins during the iron boom of 2012–2015. They were placed in new construction and modular housing units outside the wall, on the windy side. From the beginning, they were a separate species, with the lack of con-nectivity and accountability inherent in a transient working pop-ulation. But they're gone now. And what's left is the core group of a couple thousand people who've been there since the beginning.

They came in their early twenties with young brides and preg-nant wives and tiny tots. Now, they've dug forty-five years into the frozen ground and their sons are working alongside them, having weddings and babies of their own. They've become the foundation of a community that's become more than its minerals, more than the hole, and more than the wall.

I came to Fermont four years after I had originally planned to come. Fermont was the original inspiration for this book and for the trip around the country writing it. But Canada wouldn't take me then. I was turned away at the border. Life went on. Then life happened. And I didn't get back. But I knew I had to come.

It's been four years since I struck out northward on Thanksgiving Day, intent upon telling the stories of the people on the daily front lines of healthcare and public safety. Turned away in Jackman, Maine, I recalibrated and pushed on and never reached the end of the road.

So, now I've come. Today, I sat in the window seat of a De Havilland Dash 8, where I had an eagle-eye view of mile after mile of unspoiled, unmarred boreal black spruce forest, mantled with snow that sparkled as if to blind me at thirty thousand feet. When I landed in Labrador, I hit the ground running, dashing out in my snow boots to meet a taxi that drove me the thirty-one kilometers to Fermont. My cab driver and I bonded immediately, and he told me of his childhood here. It's clear that he's proud of this place, even though he understands the economic challenges that rise and fall here with the price of iron. He drops me at the Hotel Fermont and picks up one of the strippers getting off her two-week "hitch" and heading back to Montreal, where she lives when she's not dancing.

I take that day to walk the wall and walk the town, mostly silent, letting the Quebecois French and the arctic wind pass me. On Monday, I venture forth again, pen in hand, notebook at the ready, to talk to the people doing the work. I meet the mayor, the fire chief, the EMTs, and the doctor. I talk to the teachers, the librarians, and the bartenders. Even the mining company, ArcelorMittal, as traditionally tight-lipped as any other corporate entity, brings me into the headquarters office and answers my questions off the record.

Those industry interviews are typically cheerful, optimistic, and edited. There's a basic party line, a script to which all suit-and-tie representatives stick. Even when the suits and I put on hard hats and go traipsing through the noise and bustle, there's still a refrain of environmental or social responsibility. At first, my tour guides inevitably think I'm there to advance some anti-fracking or anti-drilling agenda. Soon, though, they believe me when I tell them that my mission is not to comment on the industry itself, whatever it may be, but rather to tell the human story behind the mine or above the oil field or among the throngs of tourists.

I never start with the company directly. I start at the firehouse. It's where I'm the most comfortable. Those are the men and women with whom I have the closest bond, the longest shared history. I knock on the man-sized door of the house, a smile on my face and a tub of ice cream in my hand, and they dutifully let me in. Then we start talking. I always start with the trucks.

We go out to the apparatus bay and I take notes on the make and model of their engines and ladders. We talk about the dimensions of their supply lines, the robustness of the town's hydrant system, the length in feet of the ladders and the pounds per square inch of the pump. We talk in gallons per minute and calls per year and the demographics of their staff. We kick the tires and look at the turnouts and open the drug box on the ambulance. They show off the diamond plate on the rigs and the brass on their chests and the radios on their hips. After they show me the kitchen and the day room and the bunkroom, we sit in one of the offices or on the tailboard of one of the trucks and they tell me the rest.

They tell me of their wives and kids, their hobbies and hunting, their brothers in the badge. They tell me about the slow times and the busy boom years and of budget cuts. They tell me about the things that hurt them. Some guy who got burned. Someone who lost his wife to cancer or lost a kid to SIDS. They tell me about why they came here or why they stay. They give me names of other people to talk to or other places to go. They tell me where to eat and where to walk. And they all sound the same.

In equal measure, each voice has both a somber note of responsibility and duty and a light note of pride and dedication. At each interview, I am simultaneously uplifted by the indomitability of honor and relieved of the fatigue I often felt when I was in their boots. My job now is easy, no matter how hungry or cold

I've been along the trip. Because my only responsibility now is my fidelity to the story. My job is to translate, to listen to what lies behind the stats and the run reports, and to find the humanity. All these miles, all these months, all the call signs and placards and slogans and official statements, prove again that our stories are universal, no matter the latitude.

To get to the firehouse in Fermont, instead of driving up to it and parking alongside the apron, I walk to it from the inside of the Mur-écran. The station is 1.3 kilometers away from my room at the Hotel Fermont. The hotel is at the eastern terminus and the station near the west. I walk into the glass foyer, past the suicide prevention sign, and announce myself to the department secretary.

There's a bit of a language barrier. Northern Quebec is exceptionally mono-lingual French, even though Fermont is much closer to English-speaking Labrador than it is to Montreal. I struggle with my high school French and she struggles with her English as a second language. In a rare moment for me, we can't seem to come together in our understanding. Our friendly, if less than comprehending, banter draws the fire chief from his office around the corner. He's one of two full-time, paid employees on the fire department here and he's called a director. He's kind and welcoming and he quickly passes me off to the captain, the other paid guy on duty.

The captain takes me into the apparatus bay, picking up the EMS supervisor along the way, and the three of us relax and shoot the shit. The captain tells me about himself while he tells me about the department. His English is only moderately better than the secretary's, so sometimes the EMS supervisor has to interpret for us.

There are twenty-eight firefighters including himself and the director. The other twenty-six folks get paid per call, of which they run about seventy-five per year. That's one or two calls a week. It's a slow department. Their compliment of two pumpers, one "straight-stick" ladder, one heavy rescue, a rehab & warming truck (converted from an old bread van), a fire prevention suburban that doubles as the director's car, a Ski-Doo, a sleigh, and a fire boat are crammed into this small three-bay station that was built in 1971 like everything else here. The trucks are spilling out into the frozen Arctic parking lot.

Soon though, before this book is in print, they'll all move to a new station, outside the Mur-écran. I can see it from here. It's Industrial Scandinavian in design and much larger in scale than 1971 could have envisioned. The captain props his steel-toed foot on the tailboard of the E-ONE one-hundred-foot straight stick and tells me how the town bought it as a showroom model that has thirty-six thousand miles and no fires on it. While there are one or two fires every year inside the Mur, none of them, yet, have required the ladder truck. They're usually small kitchen fires or trash fires.

The ladder and the pumpers all boast hard-suction hose and drop tanks (*"piscine" en Francais*), along with chainsaws for chopping a hole in the frozen lake for water, if necessary. The town of Fermont and the Mont-Wright Mine itself have a robust fire hydrant system, but there are lots of lake houses and woods camps that are lacking hydrants. Part of the Mur-écran is sprinklered, mostly the flanking arms of wood frame construction. The central portion is steel-frame but is not sprinklered. Nor are the library, the school, the basement, the parking garage, or the second-thru-sixth floors of the Hotel Fermont.

There were no fires in the year proceeding my visit, but in 1980 there was a large fire at Door 44, one of the main entrances of the place, that involved the structure of the Mur-écran itself. There are fire walls and barriers built into the windscreen at Door 7, Door 22, and Door 44, and also separating the school, the library, the town offices, and the hotel.

The captain is not one of the three firefighters here who are native Fermonters. He's been here for five years, since he was thirty years old. He came north from Gaspe, where he spent eighteen years on their department after completing the requisite training at the provincial fire school. It's required education for anybody working in a city of more than two hundred thousand people in Canada. In towns of more than twenty-five thousand but less than two hundred thousand, crews undergo Firefighter I and Firefighter II training, which is equivalent to any mid-sized US city's fire academy. Smaller places, with fewer than twenty-five thousand people, send their firefighters through a regional Firefighter I course and complete the rest of the training in-house.

At thirty-five, the captain falls in the middle of the age range for Fermont's Bravest, who are twenty-three to fifty-nine years old at the time of my visit. The oldest, the director, has thirty-five years of experience and was an integral part of the six years of planning and advocacy it took to get the new station built, a dream that is mere weeks from fruition. The captain hates the big city, loves the rural lifestyle, and came here to hunt, fish, and run his dogs in winter. "I like to work," he says. "But I also love my family and this lifestyle."

In the kind of irony that I no longer find shocking in this industry, his wife, a nurse at the tiny hospital here, was severely burned in an accident last year. As with all burn patients here, she was flown to Montreal, where she spent months recovering. Any significant illness or injury here gets stabilized and then transferred, weather permitting, to Quebec City or Montreal by fixed-wing air ambulance. Given the distances in this frozen part of the world, helicopters are rarely used for transport.

There is a provincial air ambulance that lands at Wabush and ferries patients to Labrador City in the east, Sept Isles in the south, or, if they're sick enough, Montreal or Quebec City, whichever is the home of the patient's family. This is a young town full of young, able-bodied workers, like other company towns. If you're too old or too sick to work, you're politely escorted to your home in the south so that your company house can be occupied by another worker's family.

The hospital juts off the far western end of the Mur-écran and sits up on a small hill with a view of the newer parts of town. The ambulance has an interior bay to pull fully inside, so that the transfer of the sick doesn't have to happen in the frigid outside air. Inside the white building, which is owned by the province and open 24/7, 365, there are five patient beds. Two of those are general admission beds, two are for short-term observation, and one is a palliative care or hospice bed. There is an excruciatingly small but bright and spotless emergency area that includes a room for exams and minor procedures and looks like any standard doctor's office exam room. There's a small central nurse's desk that serves the whole hospital, and one large emergency bay that is labeled "Reanimation Room."

The equipment here is old and basic, but sturdy and proven. There is a single, fixed X-ray machine but no moveable scope and no CT scanner or MRI. There's a Wood's lamp for simple eye examinations, mostly looking for foreign bodies. There's a basic lab to run STAT tests. All other bloodwork gets sent out. There are fifteen or twenty nurses on staff, most of whom live in Fermont. There are seven physicians who rotate through in a three-week-on/three-week-off schedule, all of whom fly in from their homes in the south. Until a few years ago, they all lived here.

Most of the doctors have been working here for more than ten years. They're drawn to it for the same reasons the medics and the firefighters are. They like the challenge of the work environment. They enjoy the teamwork and collaborative spirit. And they enjoy getting to know their patients. None of the docs are born Fermonters; the town is too young for that. But within the next five to ten years, there will be Fermonters who are old enough to have finished med school, completed training, and gained enough experience in the busy south to be ready for the autonomy of a job like this one.

The closest help is an hour-long plane flight away on the best of days, but that hour can easily turn into three, twelve, twenty-four, or never, depending upon the weather and a pilot's willingness to fly here. There are no specialists to give advice, no surgeon, no pediatrician, no OB/GYN. Pregnant women typically return to their homes in the south in the third trimester of their pregnancies, so as not to risk having to deliver here.

Patients having heart attacks also go south. The closest cardiac catheterization lab is in Quebec City. Heart attacks here get aspirin, Plavix, and clot-busting drugs on the trip down. Given the young population base (there is only one set of grandparents here), there aren't very many heart attacks or strokes. There also aren't that many serious motor vehicle accidents within the town itself. The speed limits are low, thirty km/hour. And mine workers are shuttled to and from the site on big yellow school buses. Everything in Fermont, besides the mine, is within walking distance to everything else. The few drivers who are on the road are used to watching for pedestrians and for kids on bicycles or skis. In this close-knit population there's a little booze and a little marijuana, but not a lot of coke and no meth or heroin, yet.

Everyone has to be able to show up for work and piss clean, or they get sent home for good. And despite the suicide prevention poster I found in the town hall, the doctor on duty tells me there's very little of that here. There are lower rates of domestic violence as well. I ask him why that is. He tells me that the primary driver is that this is not a First Nation (Native Canadian) town. It is well documented that rates of domestic violence are higher in Native American and First Nationer households than in middle-class Caucasian homes. Secondly, this is a high visibility, close-knit community of people that offer each other support.

Abusers are ostracized here. And any arrest or conviction means the mine sends you home. Full-time Fermonters number about 3,000 to 3,500, a core number that has remained steady since the Mur-écran and its leeward homes were first occupied.

Currently, there are another 500 or so who fly in and fly out, 250 at a time, for their two-to-three-week hitches. During the height of the most recent spike in iron prices, the fly-in population swelled to 3,500. Modular temporary housing was installed for them outside the Mur-écran, on the windy side.

Almost everyone I meet in Fermont tells me that those people never really fit into the town, never really invested in the culture. It's a refrain I hear often in places that have endured a recent boom. The normal call volume for the provincial ambulance service here, composed of five Level II EMTs (with a more restricted scope than an American paramedic), is about three calls per month, or about forty per year. During the boom, that jumped to twenty-five calls per month, mostly at the pop-up worker camps that were scattered into the boreal woods.

There were alcohol-induced traumatic injuries and assaults and propane-tank burns. There were older folks truly unfit for the job in this climate, contractors over the age of fifty, who couldn't secure jobs anywhere else. They had strokes and heart attacks and diabetic emergencies. That took a toll on the five people who are responsible for a mind-bogglingly huge geographic catchment area. It includes the Trans-Labrador Highway, which, by March, will be walled in with thirty feet of snow on either side. Eventually, the price of iron went back down, and the fly-ins went south.

There's another group of folks who are obligated to go south. The dead. There is no cemetery in Fermont, no funeral home or medical examiner or crematory. The town planners didn't include a cemetery, on purpose. People didn't want it. The town was designed for the living, the working. And the architects knew that everyone would want to be buried at "home" in southern Quebec, from which they had come to be a part of this new social engineering experiment.

The experiment was a far greater success than anyone could have predicted. Fermonters love life here, now more than ever. The 380 bachelor apartments in the windscreen and the 380 family homes within its leeward shadow have never sat empty. In fact, at times they've burst at the seams and been sub-divided to accommodate more people. The "children" of Fermont are my age, grown adults approaching middle-age, with their own children, and they can't recall any home other than this. There are grandchildren now. The last thing the founding citizens want is to leave behind their friends and their families, even though they knew that was part of the deal when they came. A few people asked to be buried here. So, the town decided to accommodate them.

When the new fire station was built, forty paces north of the windward side of the Mur-écran, a small park was constructed west of it. Smaller than the infield of a Little League baseball diamond, it's backed by the ubiquitous black spruce out of which the town was carved. There are four rather ornate concrete benches, virtually buried in snow. I walk toward them, kicking snow to mid-thigh, and making what seem like the only footprints of this winter.

In the center of the park, amidst the benches, is a square case about shoulder high and about as wide on each side as the breadth of my arms. It looks like a chunk of post office boxes stuck out in the snow, but it's no such thing. It's sturdy, made of granite and hardwood and steel. It's stately, dignified, and somber. It's the town mausoleum and it's only a few months old at the time of my visit. Of the thirty-six spaces inside, three are filled. Each inhabitant, apparently, patiently awaited this construction, convalescing the early years of their demise on someone's mantelpiece before being transferred here.

I was directed here by the suit-and-tie guy representing ArcelorMittal, the mining company. He broke away from the script when he started to talk about his own life here. "You know your neighbor and you know your neighborhood," he said. "But if you need to be close to your parents and grandparents, you can't live here."

He finds it becoming harder to recruit young, whole families to live here, especially in the digital age. "Young people want things instantly. And that can't happen in Fermont."

Fermont is too far for things to come quickly. You have to plan ahead and may have to wait weeks or months or until next summer before your catalogue order or your Amazon order arrives. The other challenge is that more young women have careers of their own now, and unless they're working in the mine too, there just aren't a lot of employment opportunities here. So they have to quit their jobs and come here to be homemakers.

"That was the deal in 1974," he tells me. But shifting priorities make that less attractive for many women. For the people who do come here, either alone or as a family unit, they are quickly adopted by a generous town. "If you have a problem, you never have to figure it out alone."

This man, a company administrator, will be retiring soon and he's happy and sad about it. He's happy that he'll have more time to fish and hunt, time to relax. But he's sad to leave his friends and the Fermont way of life. "We came here to live here. You can't live somewhere for thirty-five years and not be sad to leave it."

It's easy here in Fermont. There's no traffic, no serious crime. There's always work. It's safe for the kids. Mont-Wright is one of the biggest mines in Canada, but it's small in the world. Together, they've moved 25 million tons of iron. And while that's a drop in the bucket for the world, it's everything to everyone in Fermont.

A Forty, A Fence, and the Town That Isn't Quite

The next generation of social engineering along the Mexican border
Santa Teresa, New Mexico. Late spring.

Before I had traveled North America, there was a time that I would have been afraid to walk into Chope's by myself. But not anymore. Chope's is a bar and restaurant in a series of adobe and cinder block buildings along old Highway 28 in La Mesa, New Mexico. It's mostly a biker bar, set amongst the onion fields and the orchards of pecan trees that are so vast they can be seen from space. Highway 28 was the old route from El Paso, Texas, to points north in New Mexico. It runs from that unique place where Mexico, New Mexico, and Texas all come together, up through the Rio Grande Valley to Mesilla (muh-SEE-uh). This is the stomping grounds of Billy the Kid, Wyatt Earp, and anyone on the Butterfield Stage line.

La Mesa, where Chope and Lupe lived at the turn of the century, is farm country. The chocolate brown dirt is flood-irrigated off both the nearby Rio Grande and the deep desert aquifers that store what scant rain they can. Here in the windy spring, the onion fields are greening, the chile fields have been properly tilled, and thousands of pecan trees have the first of small, pollen-streaming buds on them. Inside Chope's on a Friday night, the local inhabitants are, themselves, getting properly tilled.

It's been a long week for this lower-middle-class crowd of folks, so the mood is boisterous and light. It's early yet, so the spirit is peaceful. Chope's, around since 1909 and a speakeasy during prohibition, is no stranger to violence and mayhem. That's evidenced by the armed security guard outside the front door who checked my ID and snapped a Facebook photo for me with his .45 on his hip and black leather gloves on his hands.

Though I'm a bit younger than most of the crowd, and one of the only White people inside, I'm welcomed at a humble table where I can sit with my back to the wall. I spend the night learning about my tablemates, all from La Mesa and old high school friends. At the end of the night a nice Hispanic man takes me for a spin on his Harley-Davidson Fat Boy, looking very much a stereotype with his black bandana low over his forehead and his cowboy boots on for easy shifting.

It's dark now, much cooler than the day, a canopy of stars above us and the faintest dwindling light behind the western mesa. It's easy to tell which of the fields are being irrigated, because the air temperature drops about eight degrees as we ride past them. That's something I've always loved about riding Highway 28. In the dead heat of summer, the fully leafed-out pecans form a darkened tunnel over the gently winding two-lane road. When you ride into it from the bright sunlight, it's instantly at least ten degrees cooler, an oasis of shade in an unforgiving light.

I used to ride this road with my friend John. This man I'm wrapped around tonight knew him too. John was all of the people in this book. He was the absolute best of us, the epitome of sacrifice and duty and honor. And he died in that service in a helicopter crash just over the mountains to our east. He was a young man about to be a father. My new biker friend and I had lifted a glass to him at Chope's earlier. That act, in itself, was a subtle reminder that things are always changing.

For years, one kitschy catch of Chope's was that they served beer in forty-ounce bottles, both in the bar and in the restaurant. It was great fun to sit with your friends at a civilized dinner, while everyone had a glass bottle of some terrible beer, forty ounces high, sitting in front of them. It sounds like a silly thing, but everyone from this area knows about it. Having a "forty" was the thing to do here. And that, then, is the crux of what makes community. Not the beer itself, but the way we come together to drink it.

In Pie Town, New Mexico, we have an obligatory slice of pie. In New York, we have a slice of pizza. In Seattle, a cup of coffee. In Maine, a lobster. If we can't have a forty at Chope's, it's almost like we never went there at all.

Every town has something that makes it a town. La Mesa isn't much, but a lot of visitors and a lot of money have trekked west, off of I-10, just to have a forty at Chope's. And on my way through, it was a moment to wax nostalgic and remember why I'd come home. But I can't get a forty here anymore. Twenty-two ounces is the new max, as dictated by state liquor laws. Other than that, nothing has changed.

But south of here, things are changing. It's hard to see, but it's happening. Santa Teresa, New Mexico, is a small, unincorporated community at the extreme southern end of Dona Ana County, along both the Texas and Mexican borders. It's called a census designated place (CDP). It's not a town.

A CDP is a "concentration of population . . . for statistical purposes only . . . [which has] . . . no legal status." It's not a town. But Santa Teresans are Santa Teresans, all 4,500 of them. Their community has as much identity to them as any other. And it's one of the places at the epicenter of border politics and global trade.

Santa Teresa sits just north and west of El Paso. El Paso has long been a major port of entry by land and by rail into the United States from Mexico. A large chunk of North America's commerce passes through it, crossing over the Rio Grande on foot, by car, and by intermodal truck, where containers are plucked from trains on which they were loaded at the seaport of Long Beach, California. The two existing El Paso border crossings are so crowded, old, and congested that the local traffic report always includes estimated border wait times for crossing the Bridge of the Americas.

Santa Teresa built a port of entry in 1992 to ease the pressure on the El Paso crossings. Since then, it's undergone a number of upgrades including a massive rail expansion project. The old tracks in geographically landlocked El Paso could no longer handle the width, speed, or volume of modern trains and their intermodal cargo. Santa Teresa, on the other hand, has thousands of acres of wide-open, flat, desert mesa on which to develop. And that's what drew me.

Union Pacific Railroad partnered with the Mesilla Valley Economic Development Alliance to build the 225-acre, 5-million-square-foot Santa Teresa Intermodal Park and the adjacent 230-acre Bi-National Industrial Park that encompasses the Port of San Jeronimo across the Mexican border. Santa Teresa and San Jeronimo are both considered 'inland ports," and are equidistant from Houston, Texas, and Long Beach, California. San Jeronimo is home to a massive industrial building belonging to the electronics manufacturer Foxconn and is Mexico's largest manufacturing facility. Millions of Americans use desktops, laptops, and iPhones every day that are assembled in San Jeronimo, cleared in-warehouse by embedded US Customs agents, and expedited across the border into New Mexico, onto I-10, and off to the rest of the Lower Forty-eight.

Ships can offload cargo from Asia in Long Beach and get it to Houston over the rails, then back on another ship, without having to traverse the Panama Canal. The freight lines that start here also extend north to Chicago and beyond. There is an adjacent airport and an intermodal trucking facility, including a FedEx hub. There are enormous storage facilities, including fifty-three acres of wind turbine blades, all lying down and awaiting their oversize load escorts to take them to America's windy plains.

Santa Teresa in 2018 is equivalent to Fermont, Quebec, in 1969. Few who live here know it, but plans have already been drawn, debated, redrawn, rehashed, re-gnashed, and redrawn again for a revolutionary new transborder, binational triad of towns. There are committees of sociologists, anthropologists, logisticians, bankers, real estate experts, architects, public safety personnel, transportation engineers, conservationists, and hydrologists who've collaborated with universities like Harvard to try and engineer a town that's going to create and sustain a way of life and a culture.

Juarez and El Paso are both infamous for their gangs and drug cartels. As it stands today, workers in the *maquiladoras* (factories) must commute 1.5–2 hours each way to work at the manufacturing jobs that lie along the border in special economic zones that were established in the 1960s. The maquiladoras import raw materials and equipment on a duty-free or tariff-reduced basis and then process or assemble those materials into marketable goods that then go back across the border.

The majority of workers in these assembly-line warehouses are women. And four hours of commuting per day means four hours more, per day, that children are left at home unsupervised. Kidnappings, rapes, and murders have occurred on the roads to and from the maquiladoras. Mass graves of unidentified workers have been discovered out in the lonely desert. It's work, but it's far from ideal. It's truly no country for old women.

Without leadership, without mentorship or direction, children can grow discontented. They can grow into teenagers who are more easily co-opted into the drug trade and all the horror associated with it. While that's a vast oversimplification of the problem, the absence of parental figures nonetheless contributes to social instability. These new communities, still mostly just blueprints and PowerPoint slides, will be designed to keep the work closer to the home and families closer to each other.

Mexico City is bursting at the seams with intellectuals, scientists, engineers, and artists who want to do the more sophisticated work that happens in these special economic zones. But they don't want to live in Juarez. As both Juarez and El Paso have become incrementally more peaceful over the past five to ten years, that sentiment is slowly changing. And projects like the Bi-National Park are hoping to draw young, talented, educated professionals to the region, to start their families, and to stay. The sun of hope and revitalization is rising, and the future of Santa Teresa is part of that.

It's not just a CAD drawing. Parts of the invisible infrastructure of the coming town have already been laid down. The roof of that structure is what I park on when I go to see the border fence. Having driven as far south as I can without being obligated to enter the border patrol checkpoint, I turn west into the sand. This part of the state is dry and flat. Santa Teresa sits up on a small mesa that, once I'm atop it, makes it difficult to see very far or get any perspective of how the place is laid out. I need a helicopter view to be able to make any sense of it.

There's so much coarse sand that it blows into dunes and drifts that soak up the seeds of cactus and yucca, each growing only a few feet tall and sucking as much moisture out of the ground as they can. Where I stand now, that's virtually all there is, hot sand, thorny yucca plants, and prickly-pear cactus. It's pleasant enough, today, with only a little breeze and only the high seventies on the thermometer. But in a few weeks, it will brutalize.

In the summertime, the scorching sun gives no respite. The breeze gives no breath. And every milliliter of water is drunk by the roots of the sharpest stinging plants and scurrying scorpions. It's mild enough now that I can walk a bit. And it's weird. It's not a town. But it looks like it's just about to be a town. There are a few city blocks worth of paved streets with concrete curbing. There are fire hydrants and water mains and sewer manholes and stop signs. Some of the intersections have green street signs with international names on them. In others, these have already been stolen.

These are nice streets. The intersections are all rebar concrete. But they all go nowhere, each abruptly ending in a concrete drop-off with uncut rebar jutting out into the sand. There are no buildings. There are no property markers. There are no real estate signs or fences or power lines. There's just a grid of streets, ghostly and already with fading paint on the hydrants. Here and there, water from late summer monsoons has already undermined the curbing and it lies broken off and dangling. There are no streetlights. There is only sand, cactus, wind, and the unforgiving sun.

And the fence.

The southern US border has been well secured in these parts for a long time. There's been a wall. There's been chain-link fence and barbed wire and steel in several permutations. The idea of a wall is nothing new here. But this wall in front of me now is new to me. It was built under the Obama administration, and it sprung up while I was away. Though I've lived near the border for the majority of my life, I've never really interacted with the wall itself, as is the case for most of us here. And certainly, I've never approached it with the intent with which I approach it now.

This about-to-be-a-town will have planned infrastructure designed to keep parents closer to kids, families closer to home, and the community closer in unity. It will include public safety buildings, hospitals, clinics, and a new crop of caregivers-in-arms to rival those of whom I've already written.

Those men and women in uniform are probably in junior high and high school as I write this. And one day, they'll find that experience or that person who inspires them to the service and they'll sign up and get accepted and train and burst forth upon Santa Teresa with polished boots and altruistic hearts. And then, like me, they'll answer a thousand calls, and they'll see the very good and the very, very bad about the world and its humans. Some of them won't survive it. Some of them will. And maybe one of them will come to this dead-end cul-de-sac in the desert, up against the border wall, replete then with a couple decades of life and houses and families and death. And they'll wonder, as I do, at how they came to stand in this very place in this very moment, the warm wind across their crow's feet and through the salty hair on their heads.

I'm quiet enough as I approach the wall that I can hear the wall talking to me. "The wall" here is a fence, see-through, but tightly woven. It's some sort of steel that's a maroon-rusted darkness now. I don't know if it started that color or was a muted silver that rusted and weathered to this tone. It's tall. It's modestly three-dimensional and sectional. There are thick uprights, driven six feet or more into the sand, sturdy cross-members, and a stout cross-hatching that permits light and air but would prevent any significant transfer of "goods" through its wires. If I wanted to pass a lollipop to the other side, I couldn't. If I wanted to touch another hand across it, it would only be a fingertip. And to pass a kiss would be merely the passage of breath.

It's hard. It's sturdy. I can't move it at all, no matter how much I push or pull. My feet sink into the sand like I'm on a deep, wave-washed beach with the water pulling the grains from beneath me. It's only me here. No one else.

Then I hear it. The wailing. The shrieking. The keening. It comes at me from the west, from my right, and it takes me a while to realize what it is. Initially, I think it's the border patrol patrolling the fence line on an ATV or approaching on the dirt track alongside me. But the ATV doesn't come. Then I think maybe it's a helicopter, coming low into Fort Bliss, like my friend John's did before it screwed into the desert at two hundred forty miles per hour. Then I think it could be coyotes, blood-lusted after a jackrabbit.

It is none of those things. It is the fence. A cacophony approaches, like a vibration that isn't a vibration, like music that isn't music, a voice that isn't a voice. It's loud, unavoidable. And then it passes. Then comes the driving wind. Then all is still. After some seconds, it comes again, the noise, arising from far away west, rolling like a freight train toward me, singing around me so that I am caught up in it, then passing to the east. Thereafter, again, comes the wind. Then the stillness.

I realize what's happening. The wind is hitting the fence miles away from me and making the whole thing vibrate at a level so deep that I can't feel it with my fingers. That vibration within the steel itself makes a sound that comes to my ear before the wind comes to my skin. This, then, is the breath of the wall. It breathes. It breathes. It sings. And almost seems to cry.

The crying probably isn't in the wall. It's in me. It's in my head. Deep, deep in the bone box up there. It's everything I've heard, the screaming of women in labor who, in the most absolute of desperation, walked across this desert border, in full-blown, about-to-drop labor, to have their babies amidst the sand and the scorpions, to come screaming into my waiting arms and gloved hands, so that they might have a glimmer of a chance at life as an American citizen.

Their cries reverberate in this very land of blood and love. Why would any woman subject herself to that, if not for love and hope? I hated it then. I hate it still. I hate the suffering and the sacrifice and these arbitrary lines in the original sand. But I did what I could. And I do what I can. Today, what I can do is tell stories. I can translate this vibration into the voice of a human, a real person, made up of the same carbon and nitrogen that also makes me.

We all come from this dirt. This dirt came from those stars. And through all our blood courses the iron, the magnesium, and the sodium of the Big Bang. We eat this dirt and the plants and animals that grow in it. We drink this hydrogen condensed from the air I'm breathing. And we sweat it out and piss it out and cry it out in tears that fall like rain to wet that same dirt so something else can grow. Someday, this ground will get the nitrogen and the carbon of my body. And from it, something will grow. That, then, is the story. It's all our stories.

I've come back to this place I've always known I'd be buried. Older. Grayer. Harder. But also demonstrably softer. And this place on the Rio Grande, next to this gossamer and ridiculous wall, welcomes me like I never left. I'll always hear the screams here. But I also hear the laughter. I hear, "I love you." I hear, "Welcome." I hear what has been there all along, what those of us in blue shirts and steel-toes are really ever seeking. "You are part of this, and it's better for having had you."

10-8 (Available)

There's something about the wind. It always makes me restless. It's kinesthetic. Portentous. Wind alters the day and its plans. Alters the land and its slope. Changes the shape of the trees and the speed at which I walk. Wind can drive the cold into my marrow in the frozen north, or the sand into my teeth in the broiling south. Wind drives me toward shelter before rain does. It fatigues me more than snow does. It changes the calculus of everything.

I grew up in the wind. In the southeast corner of New Mexico, out on the Llano Estacado—the Staked Plains—the air roars like a lion from long before March until long after June. In the oil patch, what's lifted by the wind can brown out the sun. Tumbleweeds can choke off barbed wire fences for dozens of miles. The wind blows so hard it steals voices as soon as words leave lips.

But wind, inevitably, also carries voices along with it. I've heard them through the border wall at Santa Theresa. I've heard them across the airless gap between our earth and the low-orbit space station. I've heard them crackle over an 800 MHz radio in Alaska, and in the whining tires of the Indianapolis Motor Speedway. They've echoed off the canyon walls and the slag heaps of the mining west. They've chanted a ghostly protest in North Dakota next to the Missouri River, where lamentations have choruses for thousands of years. Where the icy road dumps into the Arctic Ocean, there was a singing of voices, salty and cold.

The wind has been with me in every extreme. In listening to it, I've learned some central tenets that I think are important to convey to my colleagues. For those of us in uniform, it's important to know that our experience is universal. That does not diminish the effect that a lifetime of trauma has on an individual psyche. But what it does is serve as comfort in the coldest, darkest nights.

We, each of us, are alone in our memories, because we each experience every call for help differently. But in that solitude, we are all together. We've each, in our turn, in our time, felt the rage that wells up when someone who's never polished a steel-toed boot spits out some platitude of well-intentioned ignorance. We've all felt like outsiders at the dinner table, surrounded by people who may love us, but who are not equipped to deal with the lability of our emotions. We've all woken up wondering whether the scream we heard came out of our own mouths, or out of our dreams. We all see the potential for disaster in what others consider mundane.

We almost all, at one time or another in our careers, will despair the species, see life as futile and contemplate our own deaths in the most vivid and graphic of scenarios. Some of us will dream of taking control of that death, even if we only dream it fleetingly. Still others of us will give it serious consideration and planning. And finally, some of us will act. It is that last group with whom I most closely identify. It is that last group I'm trying to reach.

I have been to the knife edge of suicidality, more than once. And it's only the tiniest of motivations that could have tipped me either way. To date, I've always tipped back toward life, however wretched or glorious it is. But I can't promise that by the time you read this, I won't be dead. Larry Brown was alive when I first read his book *On Fire* and started to want to write. Now, I write, and he's dead. Some of my friends are dead. But there are more of them who are still alive.

Since I started telling my story, my colleagues near and far have shared their own stories, their own paths through this crazy world that is emergency response. And every year, someone in uniform, somewhere, tells me that it made a difference to them to know there was another person who felt the same way they did. When we give ourselves over to our honest voices, we become a part of a community.

The easiest place to do that, to talk, is in the firehouse. Firefighters have a built-in relationship based on proximity and a shared home. So do flight crews, the pilots, the nurses, and the paramedics who arrive by air to the relief of ground crews and patients alike. It's a little less easy for the ambulance teams whose crew is smaller, usually two people. In municipal, county, and hospital-based EMS, there may not be a base or a station to speak of. And given the pace of the work and the austerity of budgets and staff, there may be no time in a twenty-four-hour shift in which to debrief with a partner.

It's harder for the cops. They're alone most of the time. Especially the rural officers of the sheriff's department, the state police, the forest service, or the border patrol; their closest partner may be half an hour away, or more. Many rural officers take their cruisers home at night, retiring to their dinner tables and marriage beds instead of to a precinct with their fellow officers. There are thousands of one-cop towns across North America, where there may be only a single officer on duty at a time. And while there's a high reliance on mutual aid response and interoperability, by nature and by allocation, each officer returns to their own jurisdiction at the completion of a shift. They hand off the cruiser to the incoming officer and finish their paperwork alone. With the nature of the job today, a few minutes of cross-commiseration during the changing of the guard is not enough to preserve mental health in law enforcement.

Dispatchers have each other, sometimes too much of each other. The alarm room is like a submarine in which every sailor is tethered to their desk by a fifteen-foot cord. Most inter-jurisdictional dispatch centers across the United States have multiple emergency operators on duty at all times. But there are a few, including Newtown, Connecticut, that staff the dispatch center with one body at a time.

On that terrible day when a psychopath shot a bunch of six-year-olds in the face, there was one person in the dispatch center inside the empty volunteer firehouse, across the street from the entrance to Sandy Hook Elementary School. In the massive police response that followed, so many law enforcement vehicles arrived at once that they choked off the "apron" or the driveway of the firehouse so thoroughly that firefighters couldn't pull their trucks out.

I cannot imagine what it was like for that dispatcher, alone in the building, trapped and unsure of where the gunman was, sitting like a duck and still responsible for answering unrelated 911 calls.

Even more isolated than those folks, the tow truck drivers have it pretty bad. Every major accident requires a tow truck. They're always needed for carting off the crumpled, the smashed, and the bloodied cars . . . the kind of cars that make bystanders look away. Sometimes, the tow truck becomes an active partner in the rescue operation. A heavy tow chain and a wench can keep a car from sliding down an embankment or falling off a bridge while firefighters and technical rescue specialists work hard to cut the metal from the flesh stuck inside it.

The tow truck, once engaged, is obligated to remain on scene until the vehicle is empty of victims and ready for transport. On a fatal accident, that means sticking it out in the heat and the cold, in the blazing sun and the starless night, until the cops have finished the death investigation. Once the car is aboard, the man (very rarely, the woman) drives away from the flashing lights and the smoking traffic flares. Alone but for the shards of glass on the floorboard and the blood on the airbag, he gets no training in trauma. He gets no chance to debrief and no recognition of the valor of his uniform. No one brings Christmas cookies to the tow truck yard and no one buys him coffee on September 11. Yet he awakens with the same visions of the dead and dying that the rest of us do after a bad wreck.

There are others like the tow operator, others who have no badge to be recognized, no crew to call family, no union to advocate for their mental health. They are the mortician and the emergency veterinarian. The medical examiner and the utility workers. It's hard for all of us. It's harder for those who are alone. My hope is that those who've read this far feel less alone. They may agree or disagree with my assessments, my observations, or the way I told the story. But at least they know the work doesn't go unobserved. And that they aren't worthless.

In the boomtowns of North America, there are men and women who walk into harm's way, every day, even as the odds are stacked against them and their communities change around them. I found a total absence of abandonment by the first responders in these towns. By their nature, they can't leave their posts. They're always available. They're always 10-8.

Acknowledgments

As with most authors, there is a team of people beside me, without whom I could not have brought this crazy idea to fruition. They've encouraged me, followed me, fed me, housed me, and bailed me out over the half-dozen years it took to write. In the coldest nights in the Arctic, a text message meant the world. In the hottest days in the desert, a cold drink and a cool place to sleep refreshed me. From coast to coast, my friends and family have been there for me.

First, I thank my mother for gifting me with her ability to write and for being the kindest of all editors. Second, I thank my father for gifting me with his gift of gab, teaching me to drive, and giving me the wilderness skills and the street smarts to cheat death on more than one occasion. Next come my second-mother and second-father, my friends Donnabeth Davis and Jeff Decareau. Anytime I've been a continent away from my parents, they've stepped in to feed me, house me, bankroll me, and scold me back into reality when necessary. There are three people who believed in my writing from the beginning: Scott Bain, Jenna Clark Jones, and Larry Vanty each supported me in a time and place when almost no one else did and told me that not only did I have a story to tell, but I had a right to tell it.

When I put out my tin can and asked people to fund my research trip, Mark and Annie Lanzieri, Brenda and Mike Hays, Vicki Behl, and Clare Stedman all filled it with nickels, even knowing I was a poor investment. They started a trend that many of my friends graciously followed, including Andrew and Darlene Chaffey, Stoney Cook, Eric Palma, Chad and Laura Zecha, Janet Behl, Kelly Behl, Mary Morgan, Andy Embury, Jed Rauscher, Rebecca Laber-Smith, Kathryn Auten, Neil Murphy, Jacqueline Fournier, Susan Thompson-Brown, Tyler Lemay, Tim Jackson, Larry Rosansky, Frank Piccioli, Cynthia Zucchero, and Gina Stoll. Katie Marchessault kept me dancing and gave me a reason to come back home.

I flopped on a lot of couches including those of John (Queso) Casal and Billie Bosh Davies, Ethan Karol, Steve Johnson, Tyler and

Stephanie Lemay, Jason Osborne, Karl and Andrea Chaffey (my original BFF), Andrew and Darlene Chaffey, Scott Bain, Paul Honeywell, Chad Zecha, Jim Herrera, Eric Palma, Anne and Dennis Behl, and Larry Rosansky.

I am grateful to James Meader, the first publisher to look at this book and reject it outright. His advice to re-write it completely was painful, but spot on. I'm lucky to have found Suzzanne Kelley and the team at North Dakota State University Press, who took a chance on a new author and made her a better writer, and this a better book. And thanks are due to my partner, Aaron Tester, who has bravely jumped in to ride shotgun on this epic trip of ours.

About the Author

Robin Lynn Behl grew up in southeastern New Mexico, where she got her first taste of emergency response as a volunteer firefighter just after she graduated from high school. That early passion for helping people was solidified during her undergraduate tenure at New Mexico State University, where she continued her service and training with Mesilla Fire Department as a firefighter and EMT. She would go on to spend thirteen years in Emergency Services with a variety of agencies around the country, becoming a paramedic and a dispatcher. She earned a master's degree in medicine at the University of New England, in Portland, Maine, and worked as a physician assistant in cardiovascular medicine for seven years.

In that time, she had the opportunity to train and work in the Arctic, both in Alaska and in Greenland. Her love for remote northern climates and her insatiable wanderlust inspired *Price Per Barrel*, her first nonfiction book. Robin was previously published in an academic journal related to her medical practice, "The Hidden Field of View: Challenges in Sustaining a Robotic Open-Heart Program."

In her travels, Robin has visited every state in the union, every province in Canada, and more than three dozen countries. She has left the practice of medicine and now works in documentary filmmaking, which allows her to tell stories in a whole new way. She is a musician, a dancer, and a choreographer who feels most at home when she's on a stage.

She is currently working on her next book, a critical look at medicine in America and what drives providers like her out of the field and into work they find more rewarding.

About the Press

North Dakota State University Press (NDSU Press) exists to stimulate and coordinate interdisciplinary regional scholarship. These regions include the Red River Valley, the state of North Dakota, the plains of North America (comprising both the Great Plains of the United States and the prairies of Canada), and comparable regions of other continents. We publish peer reviewed regional scholarship shaped by national and international events and comparative studies.

Neither topic nor discipline limits the scope of NDSU Press publications. We consider manuscripts in any field of learning. We define our scope, however, by a regional focus in accord with the press's mission. Generally, works published by NDSU Press address regional life directly, as the subject of study. Such works contribute to scholarly knowledge of region (that is, discovery of new knowledge) or to public consciousness of region (that is, dissemination of information, or interpretation of regional experience). Where regions abroad are treated, either for comparison or because of ties to those North American regions of primary concern to the press, the linkages are made plain. For nearly three-quarters of a century, NDSU Press has published substantial trade books, but the line of publications is not limited to that genre. We also publish textbooks (at any level), reference books, anthologies, reprints, papers, proceedings, and monographs. The press also considers works of poetry or fiction, provided they are established regional classics or they promise to assume landmark or reference status for the region. We select biographical or autobiographical works carefully for their prospective contribution to regional knowledge and culture. All publications, in whatever genre, are of such quality and substance as to embellish the imprint of NDSU Press.

We changed our imprint to North Dakota State University Press in January 2016. Prior to that, and since 1950, we published as the North Dakota Institute for Regional Studies Press. We continue to operate under the umbrella of the North Dakota Institute for Regional Studies, located at North Dakota State University.